W9-BDQ-286

Biblical Amnesia

A Forgotten Story of Redemption, Resistance and Renewal

Scott W. Gustafson

Copyright © 2004 by Scott W. Gustafson

All rights reserved. No part of this book shall be reproduced or transmitted in any form or by any means, electronic, mechanical, magnetic, photographic including photocopying, recording or by any information storage and retrieval system, without prior written permission of the publisher. No patent liability is assumed with respect to the use of the information contained herein. Although every precaution has been taken in the preparation of this book, the publisher and author assume no responsibility for errors or omissions. Neither is any liability assumed for damages resulting from the use of the information contained herein.

ISBN 0-7414-2175-5

Biblical quotations are from the Revised Standard Version of the Bible, copyright 1952 (2nd edition, 1971) by the Division of Christian Education of the National Council of the Churches of Christ in the United States of America. Used by permission. All rights reserved.

Published by:

PUBLISHING.COM

1094 New Dehaven Street, Suite 100
West Conshohocken, PA 19428-2713
Info@buybooksontheweb.com
www.buybooksontheweb.com
Toll-free (877) BUY BOOK
Local Phone (610) 941-9999
Fax (610) 941-9959

Printed in the United States of America

Printed on Recycled Paper

Published January 2005

For Matthew and Gregory Gustafson

That they may live abundant lives.

Table of Contents

Preface

This is an effort to develop a framework for the analysis of the Bible using the remarkably creative work of Raine Eisler, Daniel Quinn and Neil Postman. Such an undertaking might surprise those who know the work of these people because it is clear that the Bible is not their primary focus. Nonetheless, each author has more than a passing interest in things Biblical. When considered together, their work yields profound insights into the nature of the Bible and Western civilization.

Raine Eisler's *Chalice and the Blade* is of utmost importance to what follows. Using archeological evidence, she argues that human beings have ordered life in two distinct ways. She calls them the dominator model and the partnership model. The dominator model is the most recent. Its essential feature is ranking. The dominator model exists where ranking exists. Where ranking does not exist, the dominator model does not exist. According to Eisler, the ranking of men above women is the most universal form of the dominator model's ranking process. From time to time, however, the dominator model has ranked clergy above laity, white people above people of color, Europeans above Native Americans, adults above children, the rich above the poor, etc. The dominator model is, therefore, hierarchical in structure, and it uses diversity as a reason to rank one person above another.

The partnership model understands life as an interrelated web rather than as a hierarchy. Women, the ones who give life, are deemed central. This does not mean that they dominate. Understanding life as an interrelated web means that culture is "partnered" for the purpose of giving and sustaining life. The partnership model does not use life's diversity as a reason to rank one person or life form above another. Instead, the partnership model recognizes that diversity makes the task of sustaining and supporting life easier. Diversity means difference in talents and abilities. The partnership model employs these differences in the task of sustaining and supporting life. It recognizes that the more diversity that can be brought to bear on the task of nurturing life, the more likely this task is to be accomplished.

While much more will be said about the dominator model and the partnership model in this book, two things are important to note at this time. First, Eisler's archeological findings indicate that human beings lived in accord with the partnership model for thousands upon thousands of years. It was only recently (the last 8 to 10 thousand years) that the dominator model has emerged to become the way we now order our lives. Second, the Bible can be read as the earliest recorded struggle between the dominator model and the partnership model with the God of the Bible on the side of the partnership model. *In other words, Eisler's account of the struggle between the dominator model and the partnership model provides the framework through which the Bible will be analyzed in this book.*

Eisler does not give many reasons for the decline of the partnership model and the rise of the dominator model. The combined work of Daniel Quinn and Neil Postman, however, assists in this endeavor. According to Quinn, the transformation from the partnership model to the dominator model began with the agricultural revolution. In his view, the agricultural revolution did not begin when people began to plant crops. This had been done in some fashion before the agricultural revolution. Instead, the agricultural revolution was a change in the way we thought about food. For the first time, food was thought of as a commodity. It was something that could be bought and sold. Prior to the agricultural revolution, food was no more to be bought and sold than the air we breathe. After the agricultural revolution, food acquired a value independent of its value as one of life's necessities.

The commoditization of food was the premiere technology of the agricultural revolution. This assertion might sound strange to most people because most people think that technology only pertains to machines. This is not completely true. Technology also pertains to new ways of thinking about what we are doing. The innovative technology of McDonalds, for example, was not primarily related to machines. It was a new way of thinking about food preparation. To be sure, new machines were developed to assist in the efficiency of food preparation, but these machines merely served the primary technology, namely, a new way of thinking about food preparation we now call "fast food." The agricultural revolution was a similar technological development. It was a new way of thinking about food that had some dramatic social consequences.

Time and time again, Neil Postman has demonstrated that new technologies are never ideologically neutral. A new technology often dictates how we think and how we organize our social lives. When the agricultural revolution made food into a commodity, a new way of life emerged. The moment food became something that was bought and sold society developed criteria that determined who is worthy of food and who is not. Ranking began with the development and implementation of such criteria. Since ranking is the defining characteristic of the dominator model, the ideology and social structure of the dominator model emerged from the agricultural revolution's new technology, namely, the commoditization of food.

A more complete analysis will have to wait until the first chapter; however, it is important to recognize that the partnership model is not an idealistic utopian dream. In the first place, Eisler *discovers* the partnership model in human history. In other words, she argues that the partnership model successfully ordered human life for tens of thousands of years. The partnership model is not speculative philosophy. It is and was a successful way to live. Second, it is neither possible nor desirable to recover the way that primitive human beings lived their version of the partnership model. There is ample evidence to suggest that these primitive people had their problems. They killed and waged war. Life expectancy was much shorter. Food supplies were less predictable, and people were subject to the whims of nature. In saying that the struggle between the partnership model and the dominator model is the framework for our analysis of the Bible, we are not saying that faithfulness to Scripture means we should go back to our prehistoric past. What is suggested is that the Bible's struggle against the dominator model means that we should continue to developed alternatives to the dominator model.

Indeed, no one who opposed the dominator model in the Bible even dreamed of returning to the prehistoric past. They expressed their opposition by building their own versions of alternative communities. Since the Bible discloses many alternative expressions to the dominator model, the phrase "partnership ways" will replace Eisler's partnership model. Partnership ways are ways of life that are in accord with the partnership model, but the plural form expresses the fact that there are many alternatives to the dominator model. Some of these alternatives were developed in the Bible itself. Others have been created outside our Biblical heritage.

Nearly every society that has attempted to form itself in opposition to the dominator model, however, has had a tragic flaw. Each retained certain elements of the dominator model. Israel, for example, maintained a patriarchal structure. Many other efforts to form an alternative to the dominator model are similar. They are like the efforts of the Founding Fathers of the United States of America who tried to create "the land of the free" while maintaining the institution of slavery. This may be why efforts to form alternative communities are often short-lived and stand in need of constant reform.

The phrase "alternative community" has just been used to describe communities that attempt to live in accord with partnership ways. It should be noted that this phrase comes from Walter Brueggemann. He used this phrase in his book *The Prophetic Imagination* to describe the sort of community that Moses and his father-in law, Jethro, constructed in opposition to the Egypt of the Pharaohs. The use of Brueggeman's phrase also reveals my debt to his way of interpreting Biblical texts and Biblical history.

The phrase "dominator system" is also a substitute for Eisler's "dominator model" because this phrase is a better expression of the monolithic character of the social system that the Bible opposes. This phrase comes from the writings of Walter Wink whose Biblical interpretations are on par with those of Brueggemann. I find the writing of both men interesting, compelling and insightful.

Many people have helped me formulate the ideas expressed in this book. Over the past 12 years, I have led book study groups at Christ the Servant Lutheran Church in Reston, Virginia and Holy Trinity Lutheran Church in Leesburg, Virginia. Many people have blessed me with their presence in these groups, and I am very grateful to them for their insights and for their help. Barbara Brame, Susan Rhoades, Gretchen Voss, Eric Giberti, Patty Hewitt, Carl Johnson, Maria McLeroy, Rhonda Miller, Barbara Fielding, Alan Field, Marsena Field, Bernice Cissel, Carol

Boehler, Charlotte Hoglund, Phyllis Kain, Dorothy Martel, Bob Mueller, Lois Mueller, Marion Stoehr, Eldon Stoehr ,and Steve Pederson all contributed to this book in some way. I am also in debt to my colleagues in ministry who met each week for our sermon preparation. The conversations we had provided me with a great deal of insight into our common heritage. I know that I received much more than I gave in those gatherings. Many thanks go to Ken Martin, Larry Cantu, Dave Wasemann, Kimberli Lile, Bernie Boehm, Bill Zima, Jennifer Zima, Gerry Johnson and Pete Wuebbens.

Larry Cantu merits special recognition because he actually read this manuscript and offered some very good counsel concerning passages that needed clarification or, in some cases, elimination. Larry has always been a supportive colleague and friend. I deeply appreciate all he has done for me in this project and in other arenas of life. Eric Gritsch also read this manuscript and greatly aided the overall structure and design of the project. He is a former teacher and colleague of mine at the Lutheran Theological Seminary at Gettysburg. He has always stood ready to support my work. I also value his friendship very much. My wife, Brenda Lange-Gustafson, read this manuscript many times. Her criticisms and comments were clear, concise and helpful. She has always had a way of getting to the center of the issue. More than this, she has supported me in all endeavors I have undertaken in our thirty years of marriage. She is evidence of the fact that one good decision, like my decision to marry her, is often all one needs to have a wonderful life.

Finally, the book is dedicated to our sons, Matthew and Gregory Gustafson. I have written this in the hope that they will read it one day and discover that there are always alternatives to the way human beings have set up the world and that these alternatives give life.

The struggle … against power is the struggle of memory against forgetting.

Milan Kundera

The Book of Laughter and Forgetting

Introduction:

The Extent of Our Amnesia

Years ago my neighbor and I were talking about a mutual friend. We were not engaged in gossip. Actually, we were both "singing his praises." Our admiration society came to an abrupt end, however, when I said that our friend was a pretty good guy, for a Christian. This statement surprised my neighbor. Until that moment he had thought the words, "good" and "Christian" were interchangeable. He thought that a good woman was also a Christian woman. He believed that a Christian man was also a good man. For the first time in his life, he recognized that there might be a difference between good and Christian.

Since I take a perverted satisfaction in altering a person's worldview, I told my neighbor that he certainly would not have confused the word "Christian" with the word "good" if he had been a Jew or a Native American or a heretic about to be burned at the stake. Such people would be quite clear about the distinction between the two words. These people remember the violence and death that Christians have bestowed on the world in the name of God's love. They remember the destruction of entire civilizations in the name of mission. They can cite examples of Christianity's preference for the powerful over the powerless, the rich over the poor, men over women and "masters" over slaves. They know of Christian intolerance of other religions. They recognize Christianity's role in environmental exploitation, and they know how these negative features of Christianity have perversely influenced Western civilization. The irony is that only Christians themselves forget such things. We have developed a very selective memory that excludes the dark side of Christianity.

My neighbor was not defeated. He had a response, and his response was right on target. He recognized that what I had said was correct. The only trouble he had with what I said was that *I* said it. He might expect such comments from someone else, but not from me. After all, *I* was his pastor! He wondered how I could justify being a pastor if I believed such things about Christianity.

How could I preach every Sunday or teach Bible studies if I thought such things?

I responded that Christianity had not only forgotten its violent history, but its amnesia extends to nearly everything about the Biblical narrative itself. Christians remember one passage or another in order to justify a particular ideology or action, but we have no framework by which we try to analyze the whole of Scripture. We simply forget anything that does not justify the worldview of our dominant society. What we do not remember is very important. That which we do not remember stands in judgment over what we have become. That which we forget reveals both the tragedy of Christianity and the power Christianity can still bestow upon the world if its heritage can be remembered. Moreover, since Christianity is intimately linked with Western civilization, remembering what Christians have forgotten might help Western civilization promote life's perpetuation.

I ended our conversation saying that individuals had to decide for themselves if Christianity can or should continue. My suspicion is that the damage that the Christian religion has done is too great for it to be redeemed. Unfortunately for myself, I am incapable of abandoning Christianity. I am caught up in the Biblical story, but this story does not seem to be the one that Christians remember. The story I remember is about the Biblical God's struggle against the forces of domination and death. It is a story of aborted attempts to create communities that are an alternative to the monarchies and other forms of political domination. It is a story that opposes the religions of the religious ones. It is a story that is against the very sort of morality that we think our churches should teach. It is a story that opposes the exclusive and absolute religious claims that led to the events of September 11, 2001 as well as our country's response to these events. It is a story that recognizes that the spiritual is intimately related to the political. It is the Bible's forgotten story. For some reason, I remember this story. I want you to remember it too.

Remembering the Biblical Narrative

A discussion of the Bible's forgotten story is probably doomed from the start because people do not even know the basic outline of the Biblical narrative. Those who do not count themselves religious think it is an antiquated document. They do not think the events in it are relevant, and they do not think that a god would ever intervene in human life the way the God of Israel does. Those who hold such a view must realize, however, that for better or worse, the Bible has had a tremendous impact on Western civilization. Even if the God of Israel did not emancipate the Israelites from their Egyptian slavery, the fact remains that the people of Israel believe this to be true. Even if God did not deliver the Commandments to Moses, the fact remains that Christians, Muslims and Jews believe this to be so. These beliefs, mistaken or otherwise, have had a tremendous impact on civilization. One should know them for that reason alone.

Christians should also know the Biblical narrative, but most do not. In general, Christians have forgotten the chronology of Biblical events. Many think that Moses and Jesus were contemporaries. Most do not know if Moses came before or after Abraham and King David. We often confuse the Joseph who owned the multi-colored coat with Joseph the father of Jesus, and we are all quite ignorant of important Biblical dates. The following is a very rough chronology of Biblical events. It is here to help in the process of recollection. Some of the stories will be discussed in more detail later in the book.

Genesis is the first book in the Bible. It is divided into two parts. Genesis 1-11 accounts for the general situation of humanity. It includes familiar creation stories, the Garden of Eden narrative, Cain and Abel, Noah's Ark and the Tower of Babel story. This section ends with humanity dispersed and isolated.

In Genesis 12, God makes a covenant with Abraham and Abraham's descendants. Abraham and his wife Sarah have a son, Isaac. Isaac and his wife Rebecca have twin sons Jacob and Esau. For some unexplained reason, God continues the covenant with the younger son Jacob rather than his older brother, Esau. Jacob takes two wives, Leah and Rachael. Leah has 10 sons. Rachael has 2. With a couple of exceptions, the names of Jacob's 12 sons become the names of the 12 tribes of Israel.

Joseph is the first son of Jacob's favorite wife Rachael; hence, Joseph becomes Jacob's favorite son. Jacob does not think it necessary to hide his favoritism; therefore, the sons of Leah get very jealous of Joseph. They sell him into slavery. Through a long sequence of events, Joseph becomes the Egyptian Pharaoh's Prime Minister. Egypt avoids a worldwide famine by following Joseph's policies. Jacob's family, however, experiences the famine. Joseph's brothers come to Egypt in search of food. After making his brothers quite anxious about their fate, Joseph invites his family to Egypt. Jacob and his clan move to Egypt. This happened around 1750 BC.

The book of Exodus happens around 400 years later. The Pharaohs of Egypt had forgotten Joseph. They feared the number of Israelites in their midst, and, "for reasons of national security," they enslaved the descendants of Jacob. God heard their cries and sent Moses to emancipate them from their bondage. After a thrilling escape through the Red Sea (or the Sea of Reeds), the Israelites wander through the Sinai Desert for forty years. God fed them with manna dropped from heaven and gave them the Ten Commandments during these wanderings. The books of Exodus, Leviticus, Numbers and Deuteronomy tell of these wanderings and give an accounting of Israel's laws and ritual practices.

The next book in the Bible is called Joshua. It narrates how Israel took over the Promised Land, and the book of Judges, which follows, tells us that the twelve tribes of Israel organized themselves in a manner different from other nations. Unlike the monarchies that surrounded it, Israel was a decentralized confederation of tribes governed by many men and women called judges. While certain judges became politically and militarily powerful during this period, they did not become kings or queens.

This political arrangement persisted for over 200 years, but the people grew tired of this arrangement. They wanted to be like other nations. They wanted a king. They went to Samuel, Israel's high priest and last judge, and asked him to anoint a king. Samuel was not pleased with the request, but God told him to honor it. Around 1030 BC, Samuel anointed Israel's first king. His name was Saul. Saul was followed by King David who ruled from 1010 to 970 BC. The two books of Samuel narrate the rule of both Saul and David.

King Solomon followed David. Accounts of his reign are in the first eleven chapters of I Kings. Solomon reigned from 970 to 931. We are very certain about the date 931 BC. It was the end of Solomon's reign and led to the division of Solomon's kingdom into two parts. King Jeroboam ruled the Northern and more prosperous kingdom of Israel. King Rehoboam ruled the Southern Kingdom of Judah. The Northern Kingdom contained 10 of the 12 tribes of Israel. The Southern kingdom contained the remaining two tribes and Solomon's temple in Jerusalem.

One thing that Christians forget is that prophets first emerged as a separate group when the monarchy was created. Before the monarchy, a prophet and a political leader was often the same person. For example, Moses and all of the judges were prophets as well as political leaders. With the creation of the monarchy, prophets were separated from political leadership. Prophets challenged the royal worldview. Elijah is the most famous prophet. He worked during the reign of Ahab and the infamous queen Jezebel (c. 874-853 BC). Other prophets like Elisha, Amos, Hosea and Isaiah followed. Some foretold of the fall of the Northern Kingdom of Israel. This happened in the year 722 BC. Assyrian conquerors placed the 10 tribes of the Northern Kingdom in exile. These exiled tribes are lost to history. There is no evidence of their whereabouts.

The Southern Kingdom of Judah persisted until July, 587 BC when, despite the warnings of the prophets Jeremiah and Ezekiel, it was conquered by the Babylonians. The Babylonians destroyed Jerusalem and its temple. The people of Judah went into Babylonian exile. They remained in exile for at least two generations. They were allowed to return to their land when Babylon was conquered by the Persian king Cyrus in 538 BC.

The books of Ezra and Nehemiah are a disjointed account of the exile's return to Jerusalem. They rebuilt the Temple and restored the walls of Jerusalem. It was at this time that the Torah (the books of Genesis, Exodus, Leviticus, Numbers and Deuteronomy) was "discovered" and read to the people. This event established laws and codes of conduct that were thought to go back to Moses.

It is appropriate to pause in this chronology to note an important and somewhat confusing problem with Biblical language. As has been noted, the first five books of the Bible, namely, Genesis, Exodus, Leviticus, Numbers and Deuteronomy, are called the Torah. They are also called the Law of Moses, and Paul refers to them as the Law. This can lead to confusion because when we hear the word "Law" or "Torah," we only think of the Ten Commandments. While the Ten Commandments are contained in the Torah, the Torah is much more. It includes other regulations, and it includes many stories. Whenever the Law of Moses or the Law is mentioned in the following pages, the referent will be to the first five books of the Bible. This may be difficult to remember because we are so accustomed to the belief that the Law or the Law of Moses refers only to the Ten Commandments.

This brings us to the end of the Old Testament period and the beginning of what some call the Inter-Testamental period. The Persian Empire was conquered by Alexander the Great in 333 BC. Palestine came under Greek rule. After Alexander's death in 323, Palestine was ruled by the Ptolemy family from 323 to 198 and by the Seleucid family from 198 to 166. Both families were descendants of two of Alexander's generals. It is pretty clear from the literature from this period that the Jewish people did not think Alexander was as "Great" as the rest of the world seemed to think he was. The Jewish people were capable of understanding Alexander from the perspective of the vanquished rather than the victor. This perspective led them to understand the horror present within Alexander's accomplishments.

A Jewish revolt under the leadership of Judas Maccabeus reestablished Jewish rule of Palestine in 166 BC, but the land fell under Roman rule when General Pompey conquered the region in 63 BC. The Romans ruled through puppets like Herod the Great who probably ruled Palestine when Jesus was born.

The New Testament books Matthew, Mark, Luke and John are the Gospels. They give slightly differing accounts of Jesus' life. Suffice it to say, Jesus gathered disciples like Peter, James and John, but unlike most teachers in the period, a number of women, such as Mary Magdalene, were Jesus' disciples as well. Jesus' influence grew. His teaching and the miracles he performed made him both popular and a threat to the establishment. The Jewish religious leadership conspired with Roman authorities to execute Jesus. Jesus was crucified around 30 AD.

Jesus' followers claimed that Jesus rose from the dead following his crucifixion. They began to worship him as Messiah. Since the Greek word for Messiah is Christos, Jesus' followers began to call Jesus the Christ. In other words, Christ is not Jesus' last name. It is a title.

The Jewish leadership could not tolerate these people claiming that Jesus was the Messiah. They began to persecute those who made such claims. They stoned Stephen who was a deacon in the assembly of Jesus' followers. A man named Saul participated in this murder. The authorities commissioned Saul to go to Damascus and continue the persecution of those claiming that Jesus was the Messiah. On the way to Damascus, he had a conversion experience. He believed that he had encountered the risen Jesus.

This experience changed everything for Saul. He changed his name to Paul and eventually became the most effective missionary in Christian history. He believed that he was sent to the Gentiles. Gentiles are people who are not Jews. Paul's ministry to the Gentiles created the first crisis in the emerging church. Until this time, Christians had understood themselves to be a part of the Jewish faith. They knew that Jewish authorities had a hand in Jesus' crucifixion and the subsequent persecution of Jesus' followers; however, this did not mean that they rejected Judaism. On the contrary, they were Jews. Paul's ministry posed the question, "Did someone have to become a Jew before becoming a Christian?" This may have been merely a theoretical question for men who were Jewish by birth. They had been circumcised on the eighth day of their life in accord with the Torah. It was not, however, a mere theoretical problem for adult males interested in converting to Christianity. If one had to become a Jew before becoming Christian, the male converts would have to be circumcised. Needless to say, such a ceremony might make male converts think twice about conversion.

Paul won the fight to include Gentiles without first making them become Jews. This made Paul's mission to the Gentiles easier and probably much more successful. Paul may have been executed by the Romans in Rome around the year 65 AD. His ministry spanned three decades, and he wrote the New Testament letters Romans, I and II Corinthians, I Thessalonians, Galatians, Philippians, Philemon and possibly Ephesians and Colossians.

This concludes a rough chronological outline of the Biblical narrative. Christians have forgotten most of it. They are familiar with certain stories, but in most cases, they have forgotten the chronology and the contexts of these stories. A review of the approximate order of the events and knowledge of a few important dates is an important first step in this effort to counter our Biblical amnesia. If we can remember these events, we might be able to determine what is going on in the Bible. Perhaps we can then begin to make amends for the tragedy of Christianity.

Other Memories to Rekindle

Biblical content is not the only thing we have forgotten. We have forgotten that human beings lived thousands of years before the writing of the Bible. We have forgotten that life existed on this planet hundreds of millions of years before human beings, and we have forgotten that the planet existed billions of years before life emerged.

We have not exactly forgotten these things. Some Christians simply choose not to believe these facts. They think that the earth has been around for six or seven thousand years. They think they have Biblical reasons for their conclusion, but their conclusions are simply wrong. The earth is really quite old. The rest of Christianity is more dishonest with the way they handle this fact. The rest of Christianity knows that billions of years elapsed between the birth of the planet and the writing of Scripture, but they simply pretend this fact is irrelevant.[1] They pretend that the age of the earth and the time human beings have roamed the planet have absolutely no bearing on the interpretation of Scripture.

This fantasy prevents Christians from asking the crucial question, "What is the context into which Scripture was written?" We have been interpreting Scripture as if it has no context at all! The importance of this goes far beyond religious concerns. Most would agree that the Bible is an important, if not foundational, document of Western civilization. Our amnesia regarding the Bible's context, therefore, is the same as amnesia concerning the origin of civilization itself. The next chapter discusses this issue.

We have also forgotten that everything in Scripture has an historical context. Understanding this context means that one must understand the audience's situation in life. Are they rich or poor? Have they just been victorious in battle or have they been defeated? Are they children or adults? What are the social forces that are operative at the time? What has just happened in the story? What is about to happen in the story?

One must also remember who is speaking. Is the one who is speaking the God who has just emancipated slaves from Egyptian captivity, or is it the slave driver demanding fourteen hours of back-breaking labor each day? A story from the period of American slavery illustrates the importance of who is speaking.

In the 18th century, American slave owners debated plans to evangelize African slaves. One of the reasons the slave owners decided that this might be a good idea was they were having trouble with theft. Slaves were "stealing" from their owners. The owners reasoned that if their slaves became Christian, the slaves could be taught the Commandments, and the "theft" of property would be diminished. Into this context, a rather brilliant plantation slave spoke. This man said that it was impossible for him to steal from his "master." "If I take the master's ham over there in the tub and eat it, I am merely relocating his property. I have taken it out of something that was his and put it into something that was also his."[2]

With these simple words, this man demonstrates the importance of context. He shows that it is one thing for someone who has given you freedom – as the Israelites believed their God had done – to say, "You shall not steal." It is another thing for someone who has already stolen everything from you to say, "You shall not steal." The truth of even this commandment depends on who is doing the speaking. "You shall not steal" is not an absolute truth. It is not something that is true for all time. Its truth depends on the context. Its truth depends on who is speaking. The fact that Christians have forgotten that the Bible is contextual has had some disastrous consequences. People have been killed because Christians firmly believe that their doctrine is absolute. This issue will be addressed on a number of occasions in this book.

We also forget that Israel believed that it owed its existence to the Exodus event. At the very least, this means that Israel began with a political insurrection against a dominant political power. Moreover, the subsequent history of Israel suggests that the God of Israel intervened because God opposed the Egyptian social order. One can say this because of another thing we generally forget. We forget that Israel was ruled in a totally different manner than other nations for over 200 years immediately following the Exodus. Other nations had Emperors, Pharaohs and Kings. Israel was a loose confederation of 12 tribes with Judges maintaining the social order. Judges mediated disputes, and, when necessary, they organized the people to meet foreign threats.[3]

We have also forgotten that the creation of a monarchy in Israel was a negative development rather than a positive one. When the people asked their high priest Samuel to anoint a king, Samuel was extremely reluctant. Samuel eventually anointed Saul king only because God told him to do so. God comforted Samuel saying that the people were not rejecting Samuel. They were rejecting God (I Sam. 8: 1-6). If the Israelites rejected God when they submitted to the monarchy, the monarchy was obviously a negative development. We have forgotten this fact, and, accordingly, we do not have as much suspicion of the powers that govern us as we should.

Forgetting that the Bible viewed the monarchy in a nega-tive manner also prevents us from understanding that King Solomon's kingdom was much like Pharaoh's Egypt.[4] Both Solomon and Pharaoh lived in luxury. Both Solomon and Pharaoh lived at the expense of the poor. Both Solomon and Pharaoh had Hebrew slaves. Whereas the Hebrew slaves in Egypt built pyramids, the Hebrew slaves in Israel built Solomon's Temple (I Kings 5: 13). This might lead one to conclude that even building the great Temple of Solomon was not necessarily a positive development.

Viewing Israel's monarchy in a less positive way implies that we ought to be a little more critical of the Bible itself. The monarchy itself produced certain Biblical materials. Accordingly, some stories or passages are propaganda designed to support and perpetuate the monarchy. This means that there is often a tension in the Old Testament between those writing on behalf of the monarchy and those trying to be faithful to the Mosaic social experiment. This tension is present in the stories of the prophets Elijah and Elisha. We will discuss this tension in the writings of prophets like Amos, Isaiah, Hosea, Jeremiah and Ezekiel. It will be argued on the basis of the Biblical texts themselves that the Bible is an account of a struggle between two different ways of living, namely, the dominator system and partnership ways. Moreover, Israel's God is against the dominator system and sides with partnership ways. The Bible is not a presentation of eternal, absolute and unchangeable truths. The Bible is an account of God's struggle against the forces of domination. The irony and difficulty one encounters when interpreting the Bible is that sometimes the stories of God's struggle against the forces of domination are narrated by people who are agents of such domination.

These uncomfortable statements do not mean that the Bible is not inspired. The Bible is inspired because it continues to push some of us beyond what we would otherwise be. As the Spirit blows where it wills and inspires whomever it desires, so does the Bible. The Bible is not inspired because it is factually unerring.[5] The Bible is inspired because God has chosen to inspire it, and God can inspire Scripture in many ways.

There is a joke that illustrates this point. It is a very bad joke, but it is a good illustration. The joke is, "Where does a 2000 pound gorilla sleep?" The answer is, "Anywhere it wants." The same answer applies to the question, "How does God inspire Scripture?" The answer is, "Anyway God wants." Sometimes the inspiration occurs through the literal meaning of the text. Sometimes inspiration happens in other ways. It is the goal of the one who is interpreting a given text to discern the way that God has inspired the particular text. To assume that one knows how God always inspires Scripture before encountering a particular text places a huge limitation on the work of the Spirit. It is a limitation to which the Spirit seldom conforms.

Christians might want to remember one last thing. Jesus' public ministry began with the words, "The time is fulfilled. The rule of God is in your midst. Repent and believe in the good news." At the very least, repent means to stop doing what you are doing. It means to turn around because you are not on the right path. It means you are going the wrong way, and you cannot get there from here. It means that you will never reach your destination if you stay on this path because you are moving in the wrong direction. This book identifies this wrong path. It contends that we have taken the wrong path because of our Biblical amnesia. Moreover, if we remember some of what we have forgotten about the Bible, we might discover the path of repentance. This book seeks to identify characteristics of this new way and to articulate how to walk the path the Bible invites us to walk.

Chapter 1:

The Bible's Forgotten Context

The story of Adam and Eve provides an excellent clue concerning the Bible's context. It is a familiar story. God creates Adam from mud and Eve from Adam's rib. God gives the couple the task of tending to the Garden of Eden. God tells them that they can eat of any tree or plant in the Garden, but commands that they not eat of one tree under penalty of death. The serpent slowly convinces Eve to eat from the forbidden tree, and Eve has much less trouble convincing Adam to do the same. This act of disobedience introduces sin into this pristine environment, and God expels Adam and Eve from their garden paradise.

This familiar story contains many strange elements. Adam is created out of mud. Eve comes into being through the surgical removal of Adam's rib. A serpent carries on a rather logical and rational discussion with Eve. God commands that the fruit from a perfectly good tree should not be eaten, and Adam and Eve seem to have a rather intimate relationship with the deity. What is even more fascinating, however, is what we have *forgotten* about this story. We have forgotten the name of the tree that produced the forbidden fruit. Even those who actually remember the tree's name act as if the name is not important, but it is.

The Name of the Tree

It is always interesting to ask people the name of this tree. Pastors and laity, theologians and children cannot remember. Some say it was an apple tree. The more informed say it is the Tree of Knowledge. Few people can quickly recall that this tree is called "The Tree of the Knowledge of Good and Evil" (Gen. 2: 9). In other words, the Garden of Eden story begins with God telling Adam not to eat of a tree that would give him the knowledge of good and evil. The story appears to say that our moral sense – our knowledge of good and evil – is a consequence of eating fruit from this tree, and that God did not want us to have this moral sense!

This should give us pause. Most people think that the purpose of religion is to give people a moral sense. Children are sent to church and Sunday School so that they can know the difference between good and evil. Knowing such things is deemed a positive accomplishment. The Garden of Eden story, however, seems to be saying that knowledge of good and evil is a *consequence* of the first sin. The knowledge of good and evil is not a positive accomplishment. It is a negative feature of human life. No wonder we refuse to remember the name of this tree. It undermines the long established relationship between religion and morality. It is in the interest of this relationship that we forget the tree's name.

Nevertheless, this story suggests that because Adam and Eve ate fruit from the Tree of the Knowledge of Good and Evil, humanity must interpret everything in terms of good and bad, better and best, worse or worst.[1] If a person is in a grocery store selecting meat, he or she tries to determine which meat is the best meat to buy. If someone is voting for President, he or she often tries to determine which candidate is "the lesser of two evils." The Garden of Eden story suggests that there is no instance in human life where we do not make choices based on our knowledge of good and evil. Most people think that the knowledge of good and evil is a positive thing. Indeed, human beings often say that this moral sense distinguishes human beings from the rest of the animals. *The fascinating claim of the Garden of Eden story is that our moral sense is the consequence of sin. It is not the remedy for sin that we believe it is.*

In the Garden of Eden story, morality's negative quality is further augmented when one notes that eating the forbidden fruit has deadly consequences. God tells Adam and Eve, "You may eat freely of every tree of the garden, but of the tree of the knowledge of good and evil you shall not eat, for in the day that you eat of it, you shall die" (Gen.2: 16, 17). This relationship between morality and death seems far-fetched until it is examined. Such examination discloses that these ancient storytellers were not stupid. They are just ancient. The connection between morality and death is not as absurd as it appears.

The relationship between morality and death emerges when the content of morality is distinguished from the process of morality. We are more familiar with the content of morality than we are with the process of morality. The content of morality includes claims that certain things are good and right or bad and wrong as well as the reasons for such claims. Needless to say, the content of morality differs from culture to culture and from person to person. For example, one person might make the moral claim that abortion is wrong and say the reason for this claim is that no one has the right to kill another human being. Another person might make the moral claim that abortion is good because a fetus is not yet a human being and a woman has the right to decide whether or not she should have a baby. The content of one morality can, on occasion, be diametrically opposed to the content of another morality. Moral claims can be very different, and the reasoning that leads to the moral claim can be quite dissimilar.

The process of morality concerns how morality functions in culture. Whereas the content of morality differs from culture to culture, the process of morality is constant and uniform. Morality always does one thing. *Morality always draws the line between the good and bad. In drawing the line between the good and the bad, morality identifies the one(s) who can be left for dead. It also justifies "the good people" when they do not help those who morality deems bad.* In the United States of America "the work ethic" is one of our moral beacons. It states that work is good and promises that hard work will always be rewarded. A corollary is that if a person is not rewarded, the person has not worked hard enough. Thus, everyone is responsible for their own wellbeing. Those who are not well off simply have not worked hard enough. Those who are well off have earned their status. They are absolved of their responsibility for the poor because the work ethic claims that the poor are poor because they have not worked hard enough. They are not poor because of anything that the rich have done. No one is responsible for people in need. Only hard work can change their plight, and, for some reason, people in need refuse to improve their situation by hard work.

Our public policy reflects the work ethic. Our laws indicate we think we ought to be somewhat responsible for people who are unable to work. We give public assistance to such people. Our public policy, however, maintains that we are not responsible for people who can work, but choose not to work. We believe our refusal to help such people is perfectly justified. Both the Democrat and Republican parties agree that we are somewhat responsible for the people who are not capable of working. They also believe that we are not responsible for people who can work but choose not to work. Their only disagreement is on the number of people in each category. Democrats tend to think that there are more people incapable of work than the Republicans do. Both parties think that those who can work but choose not to work should be left for dead. The morality of the work ethic draws the line between people who work and people who choose not to work. It states that those who work are worthy of life, and that those who choose not to work are not.

The process of morality reveals that the Garden of Eden story may be correct when it recognizes that morality is intimately associated with death. Morality and death are forever linked because the moral process always separates those deemed worthy from those deemed unworthy. Examples of this fact abound. In ancient Palestine, Judaism drew a line separating the clean from the unclean. They often labeled sick people as unclean, and reinforced their claim with a theology that maintained that sin was at the root of illness. If a person was ill or had some other sort of infirmity, it was because that person or perhaps the person's parents had sinned.[2] Thus, confession of one's sin was the first step in recovery. If the illness lingered, the confession was not sincere enough. One marvels at how convenient this ideology was for the good and healthy people of the world. This ideology made an illness the responsibility of the one that was sick. Residue of this moral position is still among us today. If we hear that a man has lung cancer, for example, our first question is, "Did he smoke?" If the answer is yes, then we feel the man is somewhat responsible for his disease. We are less sympathetic. Our sympathy abounds, however, if it turns out that the man did not smoke. We all know that lung cancer without smoking is an injustice.

Morality also functions as a device to justify the "good people" at the expense of the poor. Herbert Spencer's theory of Social Darwinism illustrates this. Most people think that Charles Darwin coined the phrase "survival of the fittest" as a rationalization for one species' survival and another's extinction. In fact, Herbert Spencer coined this phrase in order to account for the rise of the very rich in the midst of the very poor. It is uncertain how much money Rockefeller, Carnegie and Morgan paid Spencer for his theory, but it was not enough. Social Darwinism clearly stated that these men were rich because they were the best and fittest for survival; moreover, these men secured this status when the masses were persuaded to believe Spencer's theory. The slogan, "survival of the fittest," is a "catchy" phrase. Like any good slogan, it was instrumental in securing the assent of the population.

Whenever we exercise our knowledge of good and evil, we draw a line that separates the good from the bad. Drawing this line always leaves someone for dead because this act always classifies someone as unclean, evil or unfit. The line separating the good from the bad also helps rationalize the status of the ones classified as good and absolves "the good ones" from their responsibility for those deemed unclean or bad. This is the process of morality. This process is death dealing, and it is universal to all systems of moral belief. The content of our moral beliefs differs. The process is always the same.

When we forget the name of "The Tree of the Knowledge of Good and Evil," we also forget that morality is not an altogether positive thing. This name implies that our moral sense – our knowledge of good and evil – is a *consequence* of the first sin, and that morality is not a remedy for sin. Moreover, the story declares that we are incapable of understanding anything except through the lens of good and bad, and our incapacity to understand things in any other way leads to death. *Thus our moral sense is something to be overcome. It is not something to be cultivated.* Our failure to remember this vital insight has led to a thorough misinterpretation of the Bible. The following pages attempt to interpret the Bible in accord with this vital insight into the nature of morality.

The Dominator System and Partnership Ways

People interpret the Garden of Eden story in two ways. Some think it is a factual account. They think that the Garden of Eden was an actual place. They believe that Adam and Eve were the first two human beings who were forbidden by God to eat fruit from the Tree of the Knowledge of Good and Evil. They also think that Adam and Eve actually ate from the tree and were expelled from the Garden as punishment for their disobedience.

Others think the story is a myth. Most people think that the word "myth" means false, and it does in certain contexts. In this context, however, myth is a particular type of literature or a particular kind of story. There are many kinds of literature. There are novels, newspaper articles, science fiction, legends, poetry and advertisements. They all have a certain character. We expect certain things from one type that we do not require of another. We do not, for example, require science fiction to be historically accurate. We demand that scientific publications be objective. We want our newspaper articles to narrate facts.

Myths are stories about what happened before current time began. Myths give a reason for the way things are in current time. They tell of origins. One myth might tell of how human beings received fire. Another might narrate the creation of the cosmos. Others might tell how wine came into being or why there is sexual attraction. The Garden of Eden story, for example, explains morality's origin; tells why patriarchy exists; gives a reason why women suffer pain in childbirth, and tells us why our labor is never as fruitful as it might be (Gen. 3).

There is at least one alternative to these two widely held views concerning the Garden of Eden story. It could be that the Garden of Eden story is a dim recollection of a dramatic event in human history. Thus, it is neither a factual journalistic account nor a myth. It is a vague remembrance of a nearly forgotten past. So interpreted, the Garden of Eden story might give us a hint about the time before the Bible existed.

Generally, we do not reflect upon Pre-Biblical times when we discuss the Bible. Even though we know better, we pretend that nothing of significance happened before Biblical times. This has had an unfortunate effect on Biblical interpretation in particular and on theology in general. *The fact that the human race existed for hundreds of thousands of years before the Bible was written is an extremely important fact that is not considered in our efforts to interpret the Bible.* Recalling this fact changes everything we have learned.

Raine Eisler discusses human history immediately before the emergence of the Bible in her tremendously provocative book *The Chalice and the Blade.*[3] She believes that for three or four thousand years there was a great struggle in the Middle East. This struggle ended around 1300 BC.[4] (1300 BC is near the time that Moses is said to have emancipated the Hebrews from slavery in

Egypt.) The struggle was not primarily one of combat, although it involved combat. This was a struggle for the human mind. It was a struggle between two modes of social organization that Eisler calls the dominator model and the partnership model. These are two fundamentally different ways to order human relationships, thought and life. It is Eisler's contention that human beings lived in accord with the partnership model for hundreds of thousands of years. The dominator model emerged eight to ten thousand years ago, and gradually gained control over the way human beings ordered life.

We are more familiar with the dominator system than we are with partnership ways because the dominator system has won this struggle. It has been our way of living for three or four thousand years. The essential and most fundamental characteristic of the dominator system is *ranking*.[5] The dominator system does not exist without the ranking of human beings and other forms of life. Wherever the dominator system exists, ranking exists. Where ranking does not exist, the dominator system cannot take root. Ranking is the way of life in Western civilization. White people are ranked above people of color and people of color are ranked according to their complexion. Husbands are ranked above wives, adults above children, rich above poor, clergy above laity, masters above slaves and employers above employees. We rank just about everything. I.Q. tests rank intelligence. *U.S. News and World Report* annually publishes "exclusive rankings of over 1,400 colleges and universities." We have contests that rank lawns, chili and home decoration. We find it difficult to live without determining where we are to be placed in the "order of things."

It is nearly impossible for those living under the dominator system's curse to conceive of an alternative to ranking. We act as if the basic question for human life is who will dominate whom, and we assume that we better be the ones who dominate or else we will be dominated. No one is immune. Nations seek dominance because the alternative is to be dominated. Co-workers and students wonder who among them will prove to be dominant, and the issue of dominance is often a prevailing theme within marital and familial relationships.

The dominator system also determines how we think. It tells us what thoughts are reasonable and what thoughts are foolish. During the Cold War, the dominator system told us that those who pursue a policy of mutual destruction were sober, rational thinkers while those favoring disarmament were utopian dreamers. During the civil rights movement of the 50's and 60's, African Americans were deemed "rational" and "responsible" if they did not push for rapid social change. Labels like "irrational" or "radical" were applied to people who wanted an immediate end to the evils of racial segregation. The dominator system provides language that promotes the view that the ideas, attitudes and policies that promote ranking are reasonable and sound. Since the way we use language often determines the way we think, the dominator system makes it very difficult to envision alternatives to its way of life.

Eisler describes partnership as a viable alternative to the dominator system. Of utmost importance to her analysis is the fact that partnership ways are not her invention. They are her discovery.[6] The difference between an invention and a discovery is significant. If Eisler discovered partnership ways in human history, this means that she is not talking about some utopian dream. It means that partnership ways actually happened. It means that human beings once ordered their lives in a way other than the dominator system.

Partnership ways reject ranking and are based upon the linking of human beings to each other and to other life forms. Partnership ways understand life as a web that supports, sustains and enriches all living things.[7] Partnership ways believe that diversity enriches life. Partnership ways realize that living things are not isolated one from another, but dependent on one another. Since life is seen as a web rather than as a pyramid where the "higher" life forms exploit the "lower" life forms, partnership ways ask that human beings recognize that diversity means that life is interdependent, and that it is false to claim that we can live apart from all other forms of life. To exist in the world "means that living is more than tolerance of other life forms – it is recognition that in differences there is the strength of creation and that this strength is a deliberate desire of the creator."[8]

Using archeological evidence, Eisler makes an excellent case for her belief that human beings once arranged social life according to partnership ways. She also could have cited evidence from the less distant past. Native Americans still remember and often still live in accord with their own partnership ways.

> The relationships that serve to form the unity of nature are of vastly more importance to most tribal religions. The Indian is confronted with a bountiful earth in which all things and experiences have a role to play. The task of the tribal religion. . . is to determine the proper relationship that the people of the tribe must have with other living things and to develop the self-discipline within the tribal community so that man acts harmoniously with other creatures. The world…is dominated by the presence of power, the manifestation of life energies, the whole life-flow of a creation.[9]

Partnership ways are among us still. They are not figments of the imagination. The dominator system is simply trying to eliminate them.

The Rise of the Dominator System

Eisler gives a wonderful account of the nature of the dominator system and partnership ways. She also recognizes that partnership ways gradually gave way to the dominator system, but she is much less successful in giving reasons for this paradigm shift.

> *We have nothing to go by but speculation* on how these nomadic bands grew in numbers and in ferocity and over what span of time. But . . . about seven thousand years ago, we begin to find evidence of . . . a pattern of disruption in the old Neolithic cultures in the Near East. Archaeological remains indicate clear signs of stress by this time in many territories. There is evidence of invasions, natural catastrophes, and sometimes both, causing large-scale destruction and dislocation. . . . Bit by devastating bit, a period of cultural regression and stagnation sets in.[10]

Eisler documents a profound paradigm shift from partnership ways to the dominator model. She is less clear as to how it happened. As she says, one can only speculate concerning how this paradigm shift occurred.

The work of Daniel Quinn is extremely helpful in such speculation. In a series of philosophical novels and in the book *Beyond Civilization,* Quinn notes the obvious but overlooked fact that about 8000 years ago the human race experienced a major technological revolution.[11] Today we call this the agricultural revolution. We believe that the essence of this revolution was the discovery of farming. In Quinn's view, this is only a partial truth. It is false because human beings did not begin to plant crops at this moment. We planted and harvested crops years before the agricultural revolution. *The technology that began the agricultural revolution was not the simple act of planting seeds. The actual revolution was in the way we thought about food.[12] For the first time, we thought of food as a commodity.[13] Prior to the agricultural revolution, food was no more to be "bought and sold" than the air we breathe. After the agricultural revolution, food was placed "under lock and key."[14]* The ones who produced and guarded the food had power. The ones who did not have access to food lived under the dominion of those who controlled the food supply.

The work of Neil Postman provides an important insight into all technological revolutions, including the agricultural revolution, through his recognition of the fact that a technology is never ideologically neutral.[15] All technological revolutions impose social patterns and ideologies on those who employ the technology. For example, the printing press contained within itself intellectual and social changes that would have been impossible without printing technology. The mass production of books demanded the mass production of readers. In other words, the printing press called universal education into existence. Before, the mass production of books, there was no need or opportunity for most people to read. After the mass production of books, the need and opportunity emerged. It also is clear that the printing press destroyed the authority of the medieval church by giving people access to Bibles and the opportunity to read them. For the first time, the average person could read the Bible and challenge church authority on the basis of what he or she had read. No longer did a person have to simply accept whatever the priest said. Indeed, Martin Luther could not say that baptism made all believers "priest, bishop and pope" without the near universal access to the Bible that the printing press provided.[16]

The agricultural revolution also demonstrates the truth of Postman's assertion that technologies are never ideologically or socially neutral. When the agricultural revolution made food a commodity, food became more valuable. Not only could food be eaten, it could now be used to acquire other material goods or the services (work) of others. The increased value of food led to dramatic social changes. People grew more food than they could eat. The need for excess food required more land for farming. As time went on, people got more and more militant in their quest to acquire land for farming.[17] Generally speaking, we do not consider farming to be aggressive. We think it is a peaceful enterprise; however, the aggressive nature of farming is clearly recognized by those who find themselves the victims of farming's expansion. Native Americans or others confronted with the need for land to farm did not have to be convinced about the aggression inherent in farming.[18]

Increasing the land used for farming led to a steady increase in food supply. Most people would say that the increase in food supply is an unequivocal good; however, this is not completely true. The increased food supply is problematic in two respects. The use of more and more land for food production has led to the demise of numerous living species. Life has probably become less diverse, and this may make the persistence of life a little less likely. We experience the demise of certain species in many places on the planet, but right now the destruction of the Amazon rain forest for the purpose of farming and ranching has received most press.

The population explosion is another consequence of increased food supply.[19] The human species likes to think of itself as different and special so we refrain from applying the laws of nature to ourselves. Nonetheless, it is an ecological fact that the population of a species increases whenever it has an abundance of food. When deer have more food, there are more deer. When rats have more food, there are more rats. When squirrels have more food, there are more squirrels. While we are quick to acknowledge the relationship between food and the population growth of non-human life, we are not as quick to realize that the population of human beings is also related to food supply. Ironically, the human species may be the best example of the relationship between population growth and food supply that there is. Anthropologists think that the human population was relatively stable for many thousands of years before the agricultural revolution. Our population began to increase exponentially after the agricultural revolution.

The roots of the dominator system are firmly planted in the soil of the agricultural revolution. The militant character of the dominator system gradually emerged when food became a commodity. This increased food's value. It changed from something that was merely eaten to something of value that could be exchanged for something of more value. Accordingly, more land was needed to grow food. A cycle began. More land for farming meant more food. More food increased the population. More people to feed led to more land being devoted to farming which, in turn, led to more food and more people. At first there was little if any resistance to this cycle, but as years became centuries, and centuries became millennia, the violent nature of the agricultural revolution became evident. Moreover, we have rationalized the militant nature of the dominator system to such a degree that we often cannot see an alternative to its violence. We understand violence as a "necessary evil."

The agricultural revolution could not have spawned the dominator system without one more important factor. This factor is implicit in the paradigm shift that made food a commodity. This factor is probably the most important element in understanding how we are in the position we find ourselves. The factor is this. *When we made food a commodity, we also created criteria that determined a person's worthiness to receive food.* These criteria differed from place to place, but these different criteria functioned in the same way. They drew the line that separated those worthy of food from those deemed unworthy. The drawing of the moral divide separating the worthy from the unworthy was both the first step in ranking and the emergence of morality. In other words, the new technology of the agricultural revolution, namely, the commoditization of food, demanded that distinctions be made between those worthy of food and those who were unworthy. As the Garden of Eden story suggests, we developed our knowledge of good and evil. Both morality and ranking emerged. As has been noted, ranking is the most important and fundamental feature of the dominator model. Before food became a commodity, there was no need to rank. People had different roles. Some people were more proficient in their roles than others, but such diversity was not the source of ranking. When food became a commodity, these roles were probably given relative worth, and ranking and morality were introduced.

To be sure, the criteria used to rank differed from culture to culture, but all cultures under the influence of the agricultural revolution developed one criterion or another that ranked people according to their worthiness to receive food. Religious leaders had an important role to play in this exercise. They helped rationalize the criteria their culture used to rank people. In league with those who controlled the food supply, the religious leaders were instrumental in drawing the line that separated people deemed worthy of food (and life) from people less worthy. Moreover, their holy status made it appear that God ordained the criteria that separated the worthy from the unworthy. This made arbitrary criteria seem like the way things had to be. From the beginning, religious leaders provided this most essential service to the dominator system. They were greatly rewarded for their efforts by being given great access to the food supply. It is no accident that the leadership of civilizations under the grip of the dominator model always included the religious and political elements of society. Symptomatic of the dominator system is this symbiotic relationship between religious and political leaders. This relationship persisted throughout Western civilization even though Western civilization's religion, Christianity, should have opposed the ranking of the dominator system.[20]

The dominator system owes its great success to the aggressive nature of the agricultural revolution itself. The cycle of more and more land being used to grow more and more food for more and more people continued until the entire Euro-Asian landmass came under the influence of the agricultural revolution. The people on the Euro-Asian landmass did not or could not envision an alternative to the dominator system. Accordingly, they had two options. They could assimilate into the dominant civilization, or they could die. Those promoting the values of the dominant culture would even assist them with the second option.[21]

The Euro-Asian landmass was not the only place on the planet where the agricultural revolution happened. It occurred in

24

the Americas as well. The Mayan civilization probably had an agricultural revolution a little later than the Mesopotamian civilization. Their first great cities emerged around 2000 BC on the Yucatan peninsula. The Maya flourished for 3000 years. Around 900 AD, some of the Southern cities of this civilization were abandoned, and cities to the North were left standing empty about 400 years later.[22] No one conquered the Maya. For some reason, the civilization was simply abandoned. In his article on the Maya in the *Encyclopedia Americana,* Jeremy Sablaft says that many people have tried to explain the collapse of Mayan civilization. Some cite erosion. Others hypothesize peasant revolts, disease, earthquake or insect infestation. Schloft says that these reasons are not very satisfactory, but he gives no explanation of the demise of Mayan civilization.[23]

The Maya were not the only American natives to abandon their civilizations. The Olmec built great ceremonial centers around Veracruz that appear to have been abandoned for no reason. Around 500 BC, the city of Teotihuacan was built in central Mexico. It grew to become the sixth largest city in the world. It flourished with an empire for 250 years, and then it was destroyed. Its own inhabitants probably destroyed it. When the city died, the empire died with it.[24] The Anasazi occupied the Four Corners region of the United States. They flourished around 900 AD and had a unique lifestyle in their high-rise cliff dwellings. They abandoned these dwellings around 1300 AD.

Finally, a group of people occupied the desert lands of Southern Arizona. Beginning in the first century, they built vast networks of irrigation ditches that irrigated the desert and enabled them to grow food. This irrigation system was so intricate and advanced that it connected 150 miles of irrigation ditches – some "ditches" were 25 feet wide and 15 feet deep. This huge work was abandoned in the early 1400s. The Pima Indians named the people who built, maintained and abandoned this great feat of engineering the Hohokam. In the language of the Pima tribe, Hohokam means "those who vanished."[25]

> In a very real sense, they all deserve to be called Hohokam, these strange peoples who slipped out of their magnificent robes, put aside the tools they'd used to create immortal works of art, trashed their plans for temples and pyramids,

discarded literacy, mathematics, and the most advanced calendars in the world, consigned to oblivion elaborate state religions and whole political systems . . . and melted away into whatever landscape was at hand – tropical jungles, lush plains, or high deserts. Of course, none of them actually vanished. They just took up less conspicuous ways of making a living, either by foraging or by some mixture of foraging and farming.[26]

The agricultural revolution led to the dominator system in the Americas and on the Euro-Asian landmass. The dominator system's need to rank led to the stratification of society into the wealthy who controlled the food supply and the impoverished masses whose labor made these civilizations magnificent. It is Daniel Quinn's contention that the difference between the first Americans and those in Euro-Asia is that the underclass in the Americas just walked away from their civilizations. They stopped doing what they were doing, and they walked away. The Euro-Asian underclass, on the other hand, revolted. The attacked their masters. They even overthrew a few governments, but they never just walked away. Walking away never occurred to them because they were not able to envision an alternative to the dominator system. The underclass in American civilizations could envision alternatives; so, every now and then, they walked.

There is only one small problem with Daniel Quinn's view. There actually was one underclass group in Africa that walked away from civilization. Moreover, the history of this group is as well documented as the history of any ancient people. This group is, of course, Israel. The twelve tribes of Israel were once Egyptian slaves. Legend tells us that they walked. They abandoned their posts for an unknown world. It is from their history that we can glimpse alternatives to the dominator system. The Bible records the only story of an underclass group who actually walked away from a culture in the grip of the dominator system. Sometimes they were moderately successful in carving out a different way of living. On other occasions, they understood themselves mostly in terms of the dominator system. At no time did they completely forget the belief that they had been called by God to be different from other nations. It is to an interpretation of their story from this perspective that we now turn.

Chapter 2:

Israel's Exodus

The book of Exodus is the first record of a confrontation with the dominator system. This confrontation is significant because it begins as a struggle between women who act on behalf of life and a Pharaoh whose actions are in opposition to life. It ends with the liberation of Hebrew slaves from their Egyptian captivity.

The Pharaoh's Female Adversaries

About 400 years after the book of Genesis ended, an unnamed Pharaoh ascended to the Egyptian throne. He knew nothing of how Joseph had saved Egyptian civilization. He thought the Israelites were too numerous. He believed they had become a threat to the national security of Egypt (Ex. 1: 8-10). He made slaves out of the Hebrews. They suffered under his ruthless rule. Evidently, this harsh life did not prevent these descendants of Abraham, Isaac and Jacob from being quite prolific. Their population increased. The Pharaoh became even more fearful (Ex. 1: 11-14).

The Pharaoh tried another approach. He had a meeting with Shiphrah and Puah, two midwives who helped the Hebrew women give birth. He ordered them to kill the male Hebrew babies but to allow the females to live (Ex. 1: 16). Alice Laffey asks us to note both the inequality and the irony present in this order. "Shiphrah and Puah could allow the female infants to live because women would never become powerful enough or important enough to threaten Egyptian security."[1] As is usually the case with this Pharaoh, he underestimates his opposition. Shiphrah and Puah continue to help the Hebrew women give birth.

The story of Shiphrah and Puah displays the essence of a confrontation between the dominator system and partnership ways. Childbirth is the very center of partnership ways. Assisting with childbirth is the central metaphor for a partnership way because it

27

supports life at life's most vulnerable and intimate stage. Shiphrah and Puah were living *in* the dominator system of Egypt, but they were not *of* the dominator system. They owed their allegiance to a different way of life. They lived in accord with a partnership way, and they would prove to be formidable opponents of the Pharaoh.

They did not say a word, but, at great risk to their lives, Shiphrah and Puah simply disobeyed the Pharaoh's order. They did not kill the Hebrew boys, and the Hebrew population increased. Unfortunately, an abundance of living Hebrew baby boys did not escape the Pharaoh's attention. He called Shiphrah and Puah to account. He screamed at them, "Why are you doing this! Why are you letting the boys live?" The women calmly told the Pharaoh a lie. They said that the Hebrew women are stronger than Egyptian women and give birth easily. Their babies are born before we can get there (Ex. 1: 15-19). The Pharaoh believed the lie. He probably believed it for the same reason that he ordered the boys to be killed and the girls live. He believed it because he could not envision women lying to him or being a threat to him. Those bewitched by the dominator system are often prevented from seeing someone beneath them in social status as a threat. The Pharaoh could not see the threat that Shiphrah and Puah posed to him because he thought there was no alternative to his way of understanding the world. He was wrong.[2]

The Pharaoh then tried another approach. He issued a command to all his people saying, "Every son that is born to the Hebrews you shall cast into the Nile, but you shall let every daughter live." (Ex. 1: 22). It was at this time that Moses was born. It would take the heroics of other women to keep him alive.

The story of Moses' birth is pretty well known. When Moses was born, his mother, Jochebed (unnamed in the story), hid him for three months. When she could not hide him any more, she apparently followed the Pharaoh's order to throw all male infants into the Nile. Before she followed Pharaoh's dictates, however, she made a watertight basket and placed the baby in it. She put the baby and basket in the tall grass at the edge of the river, and assigned Moses' sister, Miriam (also unnamed in this story), to keep watch. As luck or careful planning would have it, the Pharaoh's daughter found the child. The Pharaoh's daughter felt sorry for the baby boy. She wanted to keep it as her own, but she did not know how to go about doing this. The vigilant Miriam stood ready with a solution to the Princess's dilemma. Before the Princess could think, Miriam asked her if she should go and call a Hebrew woman to nurse the child *for her*. The Princess said, "Please do." So, Moses' sister went and got Moses' mother to nurse Moses. The Princess told Jochebed to take the baby and nurse him for her. The Princess then agreed to pay Jochebed for nursing Moses, Jochebed's own child (Ex. 2: 1-10). The Pharaoh's orders are disregarded. Moses is saved, and Jochebed is actually paid to do what she wanted to do in the first place.

Most people believe the Exodus story begins with Moses, but it actually begins with five women. The male babies of the Hebrews would not have survived if Shiphrah and Puah had not courageously disobeyed the direct orders of one of the most powerful men in human history. They refused to be the agents of death that the dominator system wanted them to be. They continued to practice their life giving profession. They insisted on living according to a partnership way even if such a way risked their own lives.

Moses' mother and sister also circumvent the Pharaoh. Technically, they followed the Pharaoh's command. They put the male infant into the Nile. Their genius was revealed in the place they chose to put the baby into the Nile. They chose the place where the Princess bathed and where she would find the child. Moreover, they relied on the compassion of the Princess who eventually came to raise Moses as her own child. Whether the Princess too is a hero of this story depends on how gullible she was. Did the Princess think finding a watertight basket containing a Hebrew baby boy was normal? Did a Hebrew girl normally appear immediately upon her finding the baby? Did she think that such girls always had a wet nurse on standby? If so, then the Princess was not a hero. On the other hand, the Princess could have known exactly what was happening. If so, then the Princess was as much an agent of partnership ways as Shiphrah, Puah, Miriam and Jochebed.

Finally, these stories were told without mentioning the name of the Princess or Moses' sister and mother. (The names of Moses' sister and mother are mentioned elsewhere but not here). This may reflect a tendency of those writing these stories to think that the women are inconsequential.[3] If this is true, those who wrote the story made the same mistake as the Pharaoh. Like the

Pharaoh, our writers did not think the women were significant. Like the Pharaoh, they were wrong.

The women cannot be eliminated from this story because the story did not begin in courts of the Pharaoh. It began in the Egyptian equivalent of a maternity ward. It began where life begins and were life needs the most support. It had to begin with women. The dominator system gave the Pharaoh the power to kill. The women, however, found themselves at the very center of the partnership way. Accordingly, they had the task of nurturing and supporting life. The Pharaoh's order to kill the Hebrew male babies is an attack on the very heart of partnership ways.

The author(s) demonstrate their loyalty to partnership ways in the act of writing the Exodus story, but in disregarding the names of the women in this story, the author(s) betray their ties to the dominator system. Our author(s) are trying to faithfully express the struggle that is taking place between the dominator system and partnership ways. They are trying to show that the God of Israel prefers partnership ways to the dominator system. Their problem is their ties to the dominator system prevent them from adequately expressing what Israel's God is doing in this struggle. To one degree or another, this is the difficulty of all Biblical authors. Because of their situation in life, they do not always see their God's opposition to the dominator system. Sometimes they see it relatively clearly. Sometimes they hardly understand it at all. Their situation within the dominator system is always a hindrance. Nevertheless, Israel's God is always opposed to the dominator system. Often, such opposition is expressed subtly as it is in that of the midwives or the Princess. On a number of occasions, however, this opposition is dramatically proclaimed as it is when the God of Israel is victorious over the great empire of Egypt in the Exodus event.

The Story of Moses

According to the book of Exodus, Moses spent his child-hood in his mother's household where he probably became conscious of his Hebrew identity. He spent his adolescence and early adulthood in the household of the Pharaoh. In other words, Moses grew up with the people he would later confront in the Exodus event.

As the story goes, Moses saw the plight of the Hebrew people and sympathized with their plight. One day he saw an Egyptian kill a Hebrew slave. Looking to see that no one was watching, Moses killed the Egyptian. Moses soon discovered that another Hebrew slave had observed the murder. Fearing that news of his deed would reach the Pharaoh, Moses fled Egypt (Ex. 2: 11-16). Moses ended up in Midian where he married Zipporah, the daughter of Jethro, the priest of Midian. Moses tended to his father-in-law's sheep and goats.

Many years later the Pharaoh died, but there was no change in the plight of the Hebrews. They remained in slavery. Their God heard their cry for help. Their God remembered the covenant that He had made with Abraham, Isaac and Jacob (Ex. 2: 23, 24). It was at this point that Moses came across a strange scene. While tending his father-in-law's sheep, Moses saw a burning bush. The bush was indeed burning, but it was not being consumed by the flames. Moses cautiously approached. Suddenly the bush called out to him. Moses responded. Speaking through the bush, the God of Abraham, Isaac and Jacob told Moses that He had a job for Moses. God had seen the oppression of Israel in Egypt and wanted to send Moses to lead the Israelites out of Egypt (Ex. 3: 5-10).

Moses had grown up in the household of the Pharaoh. It is likely that he knew the new Pharaoh. The new Pharaoh could have been one of Moses' playmates as a child. One might conclude that the God of Israel chose Moses for this rather formidable task because Moses had access to the Pharaoh. He could walk right into the household and talk to him. Moses, however, may have had different feelings about the matter. His experience may have suggested that a person did not just walk right into the court of the Pharaoh and request that he release his work force. The notion was farfetched. Thus, Moses did not jump at the opportunity God was giving him. He did not want the job. He presented the talking bush with a variety of reasons for his incompetence in the political arena.

First, Moses said that he was nobody. He wondered how a nobody like him go to the Pharaoh and get the Israelites out of Egypt. God assured Moses that He would be with him (Ex. 3: 11, 12). Apparently, Moses was not impressed. He asked about his role with the Hebrew slaves. He wondered how he would get the

Israelites to go along with the plan. He asked Israel's God for his name saying, "If I come to the people of Israel and say to them, 'the God of your fathers has sent me to you,' and they ask me, 'What is his name?' what shall I say to them?" (Ex. 3: 13). For the first time in the Bible, God tells someone His name. "God said to Moses, 'I am who I am.' And he said, 'Say this to the people of Israel, I am has sent me to you.'" (Ex. 3: 14). Moses objected again saying, "Suppose the Israelites do not listen to me." In answer to this objection, God gave Moses a staff that had certain powers and the ability to perform a few miracles and told Moses that if Moses performed these miracles, he would get the Israelites' attention (Ex. 4: 1-9). Next Moses objected saying that he was not the best person for the job because he was not a very good speaker. God told Moses that He would give Moses the words he needed (Ex. 4: 10-12). Finally, Moses pleaded with God to send someone else. God got angry. God allowed Moses' brother Aaron to accompany him and to speak for him. God refused to listen to further objections. He basically told Moses that He was not going to take any more of Moses' excuses, to get going. (Ex. 4: 13-17).[4] Moses reluctantly departed.

Traditionally, the call of Moses has been interpreted through the lens of the dominator system. From this perspective, Moses chosen status – or the chosen status of anyone – is God's way of helping the dominator system with the ranking process. Theologies under the influence of the dominator system differ concerning the reason for a person being chosen by God. Some assert that the chosen one(s) did something to merit the honor. Others contend that God predestined a person or group to be chosen. In either case, traditional theologies help the dominator system in its ranking process because the reason a person or group is deemed worthy or unworthy is not important to the dominator system. The only thing that is important is drawing the line that separates the worthy from the unworthy. A religion or theology that serves the dominator system always provides this important function.

The call of Moses can be interpreted apart from the dominator system. In the first place, Moses has done nothing to merit this call from God. All that has happened to him has happened because of the efforts of the women in his life. He has done little to distinguish himself. He is not very courageous, and he definitely

32

did not want the mission. Second, the reason that God called Moses for this particular task is that the cries of the Hebrew slaves caused God to remember the covenant with Abraham (Ex. 2: 24). In Genesis 12, God made a covenant with Abraham that said that through Abraham and his descendants God would bless all nations (Gen. 12: 3). This covenant violated the dominator system's understanding of religion's function. As stated above, the dominator system uses religion to draw the line separating those who are blessed from those who are not blessed. Abraham is called so that *all* nations will be blessed. No line is drawn. The purpose of Abraham's calling – the reason God chose Abraham – is for everyone to be blessed. Abraham's God would draw no line separating the blessed from the not blessed, the just from the unjust, the righteous from the unrighteous, the saint from the sinner. Abraham's religion was not useful to the dominator system because the God of Abraham promised to bless all nations through Abraham. In principle, no one was excluded from this blessing.

Moses' mission is intimately associated with God's covenant with Abraham. In emancipating the descendants of Abraham from their Egyptian captivity, God was sustaining the life of this covenant. The God of Abraham planned to rescue an alternative to the dominator system when He emancipated Israel from their Egyptian slavery.

The timing of the Exodus is very important. Most scholars think that the Exodus happened around 1300 BC. This date is very significant. Raine Eisler tells us that the last civilization of a partnership way, Crete, changed from a partnership way to the dominator system around this time.[5] It might not be a mere coincidence that Moses was chosen to emancipate the Hebrews at this time. Perhaps it is one of God's last attempts to help partnership ways at a time when they did not seem capable of resisting the dominator system. In any case, issues of election are understood in a different way if these speculations have merit.

If the theory that the human race gradually changed from partnership ways to a dominator system from the years 8000 BC to 1300 BC is accepted, a new the reason for divine intervention emerges. The old reason is well known. It states that the reason that God chose this time to intervene is because humanity reached a stage of development advanced enough to appreciate a conversation with God. Before this time we were too immature.

After this time, some human beings were developed enough to understand what God was doing. This view implies that Moses or Abraham were in some respect "better men" than those who lived before them, and that is why God was revealed to them. This theological theory has dangerous social consequences. It implies that the "called or elected ones" are on the crest of history. Accordingly, they are more "advanced" than others.[6] This belief sparked the attempted genocide of native populations when the "chosen" Christians from Europe came to the Americas. If one ethnic group thinks it is chosen by God because it is the superior group, then theology can "justify" almost any attack on people who are not chosen, hence, inferior. This is the dark side of being chosen by God. It is also how the idea of election functions within the dominator system.

If, however, the movement from partnership ways to the dominator system was a negative rather than positive development, then *Moses was not chosen because he represents the best of humanity, Moses was chosen because the situation had gotten so bad that God had to take drastic action.* One might say that life was going along pretty well before the dominator model came into existence, but a very powerful force in opposition to life emerged with the dominator system. When the dominator system achieved supremacy (around 1300 BC), God chose to intervene. This is what was happening in the Bible! It is also another way to understand why Moses and others have been chosen.

Viewed within the context of the struggle between the dominator system and partnership ways, *the Biblical God does not chose someone because that person or group represents the zenith of human progress. The Biblical God chooses people to work on behalf of life and against the dominator system. The Biblical God does not choose a person to be theologically orthodox. The Biblical God chooses people to remind others about life and living.* We have forgotten these things because the dominator system has taken over Christianity.

The Biblical God chose Moses to develop an alternative to the dominator system. He was not better than those who lived before him. Indeed, he may have been simply the right person at the wrong time. Clearly, he would have preferred to spend the rest of his life tending his father-in-law's sheep. He did otherwise, and those who seek to find an alternative to the dominator system should study Moses very carefully.

The Plagues and the Departure

The conflict between Moses and the Pharaoh was a conflict between the Pharaoh's dominator system and partnership ways. The first encounter is pretty simple. Moses and Aaron ask the Pharaoh to allow the Hebrew slaves to travel three days into the desert in order to offer sacrifices to their God. The Pharaoh does not merely deny this request. He makes the Hebrew slaves work harder. He tells the slave drivers and the Hebrew foremen that the straw for the bricks will no longer be provided. The slaves must now gather their own straw, and the same quota of bricks will still be required. The increased workload led to more violence to force the slaves to do the increased work. Moses and Aaron receive the blame for this increased workload. The Hebrew foremen tell Moses and Aaron that their request merely gave the Pharaoh and his officers an excuse to kill the Hebrews. Moses and Aaron knew that they were just following God's own orders, so Moses prayed to God asking why God has mistreated the very people He was supposed to be helping (Ex. 5).

What occurs in this scene is very typical of the dominator system. An alternative to the system is proposed. To the ears of a 21st century American, Moses' request that the Hebrew slaves be allowed to worship their God for a couple of days might not appear to be an alternative to the dominator model, but it was. An Egyptian Pharaoh was thought to be divine himself. He preserved the unalterable course of the world and cosmological events. In asking the Pharaoh to allow his slaves to worship "their God" for a few days, Moses was asking the Pharaoh to violate the unalterable way of the cosmos. The Pharaoh could not allow such worship. How could the Pharaoh allow his slaves to go off and worship their God when the Pharaoh himself thought he was their God? To remind them that he was their God, the Pharaoh made them work harder and oppressed them all the more.

This story also demonstrates that the dominator system depends on violence and oppression. The dominator system clearly prefers "the carrot to the stick," but when it feels threatened, it resorts to more violence. Slavery is already a violent act. The Pharaoh increased the violence in this case because Moses' request threatened the Pharaoh's "domestic order." No one in this story, however, recognized that the Pharaoh was the source of this additional violence because no one could envision an alternative to the Pharaoh's domination. Everyone believed the Pharaoh's way was the only way. Everyone thought his policies were the way of the entire cosmos. These policies could not be the source of violence. The source of violence had to reside somewhere other than the Pharaoh. In this case, Moses and Aaron were thought to be the source. Even the Israelite foremen accused Moses and Aaron of being this source (Ex. 5:21). They too accepted the worldview of the dominator system. The Pharaoh's world was the way things were created to be. No alternative to the established order was possible.

This phenomenon is not unique to ancient Egypt. The same thing happens in all societies that are subject to the dominator system. In the segregated American South, for example, African Americans were often accused of inciting violence in the struggle for their civil rights. In fact, they merely exposed the violence of the established order. Their actions did not allow the violence of the established order to hide behind the illusion of public tranquility and domestic order. Like the Pharaoh's Egypt, people found it difficult to envision an alternative to the Southern system. Like the Pharaoh's Egypt, the segregated South got more violent when its "order" was directly threatened. Like Pharaoh's Egypt, the South's "order" was built on the foundation of violence and oppression.[7]

Normally we are oblivious to this fact because we are under the influence of the dominator system. We tend to believe that the dominator system's way is the only possibility. It is the way things are as well as the way things will be.[8] The Hebrew foremen certainly saw things this way when they blamed the Pharaoh's oppressive policies on Moses and Aaron. Even Moses and Aaron understood things this way when they blamed the violence on God. God, however, recognized the Pharaoh as the source of the violence. God answered with the plagues.

It is fascinating to study the plague cycle from the perspective that God is attacking the dominator system. The first confrontation happens in Exodus 7: 14-24. Here Moses and Aaron turned the water in Egypt into blood. The fish in the Nile River died. The water was not fit to drink. The Egyptians had to dig along the Nile for drinking water. The Pharaoh's magicians, however, duplicated this trick. *They turned more water into blood.* In other words, their problem was even more severe *because of their action.*[9] Even though the Pharaoh's experts only made matters worse, the Pharaoh was not impressed with Aaron and Moses' efforts. After all, they had done nothing his experts could not do. The Bible says that Pharaoh's heart was hardened (Ex. 7: 13).

After seven days, the Lord told Moses to go to the Pharaoh and again repeat his demands. He told Moses that if the Pharaoh refuses, Egypt would be infested with frogs. The Pharaoh refused. Egypt was knee deep in frogs. They were everywhere. They were in the bed, ovens, rivers and sheds. They infested farms, stables, outhouses and barns. They were in the crops, trees and food. They were everywhere.

Again, the Pharaoh was not impressed because his "experts" were capable of duplicating Moses' trick. Once again, Pharaoh's "experts" merely compounded the problem. In nearly all of Daniel Quinn's writings, he notes that a characteristic of civilization is that when things go wrong, we simply do more of what is not working in the first place. If our children are not being educated, we hire more teachers to teach in the very settings that have proved to be ineffective. If our criminal justice system has broken down, we build more prisons, hire more police and appoint more judges. Whatever is not working gets our attention, however, our solution is always to do more of the same. This is because we cannot envision an alternative to the established order.

This inability to envision an alternative to the established order may be what the author(s) of Exodus meant by the phrase "the Pharaoh's heart was hardened." This phrase appears throughout the plague cycle. God tells Moses that He *will* harden the Pharaoh's heart (Ex. 7: 3). Sometimes the story says that the Pharaoh hardened his own heart (Ex. 8: 32). On other occasions, Pharaoh's heart was hardened (Ex. 11: 35), and on other occasions, it is unambiguously stated that God hardened the Pharaoh's heart (Ex. 10: 27). Whenever the phrase is used, the Pharaoh has broken a promise and refused to allow Moses to take the Hebrew slaves into the desert to worship their God.

Pharaoh's hardness of heart has been the subject of much discussion because it violates our sense of justice. If God was responsible for Pharaoh's hardness of heart, then God is responsible for everything that happened as a consequence of Pharaoh's hardness of heart. If God is responsible, logic dictates that the Pharaoh cannot be blamed.

It is clear that those who told and retold this story had no such problems. This is because the idea that God hardened the Pharaoh's heart is simply a theological interpretation of Pharaoh's amazing stubbornness. When a person who thinks within a religious framework sees Pharaoh's incredible stubbornness, he or she can only think that such stubbornness is an act of God. This is the only possible explanation for an ancient, religious thinking person who encounters something that is beyond explanation. In the plague cycle, the Pharaoh's actions are not rational. The Pharaoh is defeated at every turn, yet he does not give in. His actions are so mysterious that one might easily conclude that they could only be created by the One who created the heavens and the earth. Pharaoh's hardness of heart merely refers to the fact that the Pharaoh's excessively stubborn demeanor and his ample stupidity cannot be explained naturally. They must have a supernatural origin. Their source must be in God.

Though counted miraculous by Exodus, the Pharaoh's stubbornness is not all that unusual. As a matter of fact, it is quite common for leaders in the dominator system to be "stubborn unto death." History records many instances of great leaders who continue their course until they meet their end. Napoleon invaded Russia. Only a great Civil War ended American slavery. The United States stayed years in Viet Nam. These things occurred because leaders in the dominator system can do nothing other than what they are doing. The Pharaoh is not unusual. The Pharaoh is an archetype for the behavior of leaders in the dominator system.

The Pharaoh could not see an alternative to keeping the Hebrews in bondage. What he could see was a whole bunch of frogs. They were everywhere, and his policies had only made matters worse. His experts had doubled the number of frogs. They may have been able to create new frogs, but they sure were not able to kill them. Apparently, Pharaoh got tired of removing frogs from his underwear, so he called Moses. He told Moses to pray to his God to take away the frogs, and, in turn, he would let the people go to worship their God in the desert. As the story goes, the Lord killed all the frogs in Egypt. They died everywhere except in the Nile. Their carcasses were gathered together and piled in heaps, and, as Exodus 8: 14 says, "The land stunk."[10]

According to Pharaoh's way of thinking, a crisis had been quelled. Like most administrations under the control of the dominator system, the Pharaoh's administration probably moved from crisis to crisis. The Pharaoh probably tried to get back to normal after the frog debacle. He had to get the economy running again, so he cancelled the Hebrews' trip to the desert to worship their God. His heart was hardened.

Pharaoh's broken promise begins a new phase in the confrontation between the dominator system and partnership ways. Aaron strikes the ground with his staff and gnats (perhaps mosquitoes) fill the entire land of Egypt. Pharaoh's "experts" could not duplicate this. The Pharaoh and his experts can no longer keep up the façade of mastery.[11] They are no longer in control of the situation, and they know it. Pharaoh's experts reported that the God of Moses has done this and implied that they could do nothing about it (Ex. 8: 19). The Pharaoh did not listen to his "experts." He did nothing. He remained stubborn. His heart was hardened.

Without further discussion, another plague is unleashed. Flies cover Egypt. Moreover, God now makes a distinction between the Israelites and the Egyptians. The areas in which the Hebrews lived were spared of this and all future plagues.

The Pharaoh now does what any ruler within the dominator system would do when faced with overwhelming force. He tries to negotiate. He tells Moses that he would let the Israelites offer sacrifices to their God in Egypt. Moses rejects this offer. The Pharaoh then said that the Israelites could make their sacrifices in the desert, but they could not go very far away to do so. The Pharaoh then asked Moses to pray for him. Moses agreed. He prayed for the Pharaoh and God answered Moses' prayer. The flies and gnats disappeared. Again, the Pharaoh displayed miraculous stupidity. He broke his promise. He did not let the people of Israel go. His heart was hardened (Ex. 8: 25-32).

This refusal pushes the conflict to a deeper level. Until this point, all the plagues were simply a nuisance. They made life very difficult and extremely uncomfortable. They were not life threatening.[12] The plagues that follow are more than a nuisance. They threaten the livestock, food supply and even the children of the Egyptians. They are devastating.

Before specifically discussing the final plagues, it is frightening to note parallels between the Pharaoh's approach to the ecological disasters he encountered in this narrative and the way modern Pharaohs address contemporary ecological problems. So far, our ecological problems have been nuisances rather than immediately life threatening. In response to the hole in the ozone, we wear hats and use sunscreen to reduce cancer risk. We do not respond to the destruction of our jungles and forests. We continue the conversion of these lands for agricultural purposes in spite of the loss of entire species. When minor ecological disasters occur, we wait until they are resolved by natural forces or by clean-up crews. Then we continue doing what we were doing all along. Could it be that our hearts are as hard as the Pharaoh's heart? The reason our hearts are hardened may be the same reason the Pharaoh's heart was so hard. We, like the Pharaoh, think that there can be no alternative to the dominator system. If the answer is not within the dominator system, we, like the Pharaoh, have nothing to say.

These final plagues deal with killing. God is said to be killing animals and people. These statements often offend our theological sensitivity. God, after all, is the friend of all people. God does not seek to kill us. If these questions are placed in the context of the struggle between partnership ways and the dominator system, however, they are subject to a slightly different interpretation. These ecological disasters are a consequence of the Pharaoh's hardness of heart, and Pharaoh's hardness of heart is the consequence of the dominator system's inability to see alternatives to its one way of doing things. Had Pharaoh been able to envision alternatives, these environmental crises would not have happened. We too face environmental challenges of enormous proportions. Until now, these challenges have taken the form of mere nuisances. Soon, they may be far more devastating. Our livestock may die. Our food supply may be threatened. Our children may be struck down. If these tragic events happen, and I hope they do not, they will not be caused by God. They will be caused by our hardness of heart. We are still under the dominion of the dominator model. We cannot envision alternatives. Like the Pharaoh, we remain silent in the face of these potential disasters. The plague cycle is as much about us as it was about the Pharaoh.

The final plagues demonstrate two things. The dominator system leads to death, and there are alternatives to the dominator system.

After the Pharaoh refused to keep his promise to Israel, God told Moses that he should tell the Pharaoh that if he did not keep his promise, all the domestic animals of Egypt would acquire terrible diseases. Israel's animals, however, would be spared. When all happens as Moses said, the Pharaoh says nothing, and he does nothing. All he manages to do is ask his advisors about the status of the Israelite animals. He is told that they have been spared (Ex. 9: 1-7). Next boils and sores break out on the people and remaining animals. The Pharaoh's magicians were unable to appear before Moses because they were afflicted. The Pharaoh did nothing. His heart was hardened. He was out of options (Ex. 9: 8-12). Hail came. It destroyed Egypt's barley and flax crops, but it did not ruin the wheat. The Pharaoh promises Moses that he would let the people go if Moses would stop the hail. Moses did. Pharaoh, in a supreme act of stupidity, went back on his word again (Ex. 9: 13-35).

Moses warned Pharaoh that if he did not keep his promises, locusts would be sent, and they would eat all the vegetation in Egypt. Pharaoh's advisors intervene. They plead with Pharaoh saying, "How long are you going to let these guys give us so much trouble. Let the Israelites go and serve their God. Egypt is ruined" (Ex. 10: 7). Pharaoh decides to negotiate. He says that the men can go, but the women and children have to stay. Like all slave owners, the Pharaoh fears a slave revolt and figures that holding the women and children hostage would prevent this (Ex. 10: 10). Moses said that the women, children and livestock should all be allowed to go and worship. With that, Moses and Aaron are thrown out of the palace.

By morning, the locusts came and ate everything that the hail had not destroyed. Again, the Pharaoh asked Moses to get rid of the locusts, and he would let the Israelites go. Again, Moses did as the Pharaoh requested. Again, the Pharaoh did not let the Israelites go (Ex. 10: 1-20). The Pharaoh still could not tolerate an alternative way of life within his absolute reign.[13] This is the way of the dominator system. It proves to be a disaster.

The penultimate plague involved a thick darkness encompassing the land of Egypt for three days. The Pharaoh called Moses for negotiations. The Pharaoh was now ready to let the men, women and children go to worship their God, but they had to leave their animals behind. Moses did not agree. The Pharaoh kicked Moses and Aaron out of his presence saying that he would kill them if he ever saw them again. Negotiations terminated. They reached the point of no return.[14] As is true of all leaders of dominator systems, the Pharaoh preferred death to adjustment.

It is at this point that an alternative to the dominator system emerges. God tells Moses to address the people of Israel. The Pharaoh has excluded himself from the dialogue. God now speaks to the people of Israel. They are given a variety of instructions. They are to kill a lamb or goat and eat it. They are to sprinkle some of its blood over their doors because their God is planning on visiting one last plague on the Egyptian people. As the Pharaoh had once ordered the new born sons of Israel to be killed at birth, God would kill the firstborn male sons of all the Egyptian households. The blood sprinkled on the doors would allow the angel of death to pass over the Israelite households and spare their firstborn sons, and so it was (Ex. 12: 21-29).

That night a loud cry went up from the households of all the Egyptians. It was the same sound that God had heard from the Hebrew slaves under Egyptian oppression. In his grief, the Pharaoh told Moses that he could take the Israelites and their livestock and go into the desert to worship their God. This time the Israelites were ready to go. They left that night. In an ironic twist, the people of Egypt hastened the departure of their slaves. They gave them food, clothing and even jewelry so that the Israelites could leave in a more hasty fashion (Ex. 12: 36). In the morning, the Pharaoh had changed his mind once more. He had to do so. His power over Egypt was based on the belief that he was God. Everyone believed that he was the Supreme Being on earth. If word got out that he was allowing his slaves to worship another God in the desert, his political authority would be undermined. As has been stated, the dominator system depends on an alliance of the religious and the political forces in society. Israel's worship of another God was a threat to this alliance. Moreover, if Israel's God had actually forced the Pharaoh to allow the Israelites to worship their God, people might begin to wonder about the status of the Pharaoh's rule. The Pharaoh sent his armies after the slaves.

The Israelites saw the Pharaoh's army in pursuit. The Red Sea was before them. The Egyptian armies were closing in from the rear. The people of Israel screamed at Moses saying, "Is it because there are no graves in Egypt that you have taken us away to die in the wilderness? What have you done to us, in bringing us out of Egypt? Is not this what we said to you in Egypt, 'Let us alone and let us serve the Egyptians?' For it would have been better for us to serve the Egyptians than to die in the wilderness." (Ex. 14: 11, 12). Moses told them to go forward. He stretched out his staff. The Red Sea parted. The Israelites walked through the parted sea. The Egyptians tried to follow, but the waters covered them. The policies of the Pharaoh had come to ruin.

A new nation stood on the far bank of the Red Sea. This group was created to be an alternative to the dominant culture of Egypt. They would attempt to become a nation that was not like other nations. At first, they succeeded. Later, their success was limited. The Old Testament is a record of their successes and their failures to be an alternative to the dominator system.

Chapter 3:

Building an Alternative Community

The Maya, the Olmec or the Hohokam did not leave a record when they walked away from their great American civilizations. We do not know how they lived after they abandoned their dominator societies. The Hebrews, on the other hand, left a record. Evidence of what they did exists. The first seven books of the Bible give an account of the Hebrew attempt to form a community that was an alternative to the dominator system they had encountered in their Egyptian enslavement.[1]

Jethro's Administrative Reform

There was a profound change in the structure of the Israelite community immediately after their escape from Egypt. Exodus 18 tells a story of a visit from Moses' father-in-law, Jethro. He came to deliver Moses' wife, Zipporah, and their two sons, Gershom and Eliezer. Jethro soon saw how Moses spent nearly all his time settling disputes between the people. Jethro asked Moses why he was doing all this work alone. Moses told him that he had to do this because the people come to him to learn God's will. Jethro listened and replied as only a father-in-law would. "What you are doing is not good. You and the people with you will wear yourselves out, for the thing is too heavy for you; you are not able to perform it alone." (Ex. 18: 17, 18) Jethro then told Moses to take his advice and appoint leaders among the people. Some should judge over a thousand people. Others should judge over hundreds, fifties and tens. These judges should address some of the easier disputes. Moses would only hear the difficult cases. Jethro went home when he saw his plan implemented (Ex. 18: 13-27).

No one has adequately appreciated Jethro's contribution to Israel's communal life. This could be because we know quite well the organizational theory Jethro proposed. We call it "delegation of power." It is a very well known organizational theory that

44

receives more lip service than actual implementation. Our familiarity with the theory, however, may prevent us from seeing how novel and innovative this structure was when Jethro first gave it life.

Israel needed a new organizational structure because they were doing a new thing. They were creating a way of life that was an alternative to the dominator system. Before Jethro's suggestion, Moses used the Pharaoh's leadership style. He made all the decisions. He intervened in the lives of the people in a big way. He was probably even more involved in the details of individual's lives than the Pharaoh had been. Jethro understood that this centralized structure was incompatible with Israel's mission. An alternative community cannot be governed the same way as Pharaoh's Egypt.

Jethro began his critique of Moses' administrative design with the words, "What you are doing *is not good.*" This echoes a phrase in Genesis 2: 18 when God says, "It *is not good* that the man should live alone." According to Claus Westermann, "Good in this context does not mean some sort of objective judgment, a judgment given according to already fixed and objective standards. It is rather this: it is good or suited for the purpose for which it is being prepared; it corresponds to its goal."[2] If something *is not good*, then that thing is not suited for the purpose for which it is intended. When God says, "It *is not good* that the man should live alone," God is saying that if Adam is alone, he is not suited for the purpose God intended.[3] In saying, "What you are doing *is not good,*" Jethro said the same thing about Moses' leadership style. Moses' leadership style might be good for the purposes of the Pharaoh, but it is incompatible with the purpose of the alternative community that these emancipated slaves desired to create. A different way of ordering society had to be developed.

Jethro, a non-Israelite, is credited with designing this new social order. It came to be called the system of Judges. It lasted for almost 250 years. For two and a half centuries, Israel was a confederation of tribes. They were not like other nations, and they knew it. They did not have a Pharaoh. They did not have a king. They had judges. They created a new social order that, for a time, was an alternative to the dominator system.

The Commandments

Moses climbed Mt. Sinai to receive the Commandments immediately following Jethro's administrative revolution. This is an extremely significant literary fact. The most important questions to address in any communication event are: who is being addressed and who is doing the speaking. The Israel being addressed was not an Israel ruled by one person. Certainly, Moses was clearly the most influential person; however, Moses was not an absolute dictator. He had already trained the judges, and the judges made judgments based on their training. The judges, as well as Moses, would decide how to interpret the commandments and other ordinances among the twelve tribes of Israel.

Who speaks these Commandments is also an important consideration. Indeed, it is so important that we are informed of the identity of the one speaking before the actual commandments are uttered. The 12 tribes of Israel hear that the one who liberated them from their Egyptian captivity is speaking when they hear, "I am the Lord Your God who brought you out of Egypt."

The one who speaks the commandment is of utmost importance. Any oppressor or agent of the dominator system can utter the same words. They can say, "You shall not steal" or "You shall not kill," but when such people speak these words, they only reinforce the dominator system. This is why the preamble is very important. It identifies the speaker as the one who emancipated these tribes from Egyptian slavery. Therefore, the commandments that follow will be consistent with this emancipation. Interpretations that merely perpetuate the conditions of slavery are not faithful to the one who is speaking. It was the God who liberated the 12 tribes of Israel from their Egyptian captivity who spoke the following:

> I am the Lord your God who emancipated you
> from slavery in Egypt.
>
> You shall have no other Gods before me.
>
> Do not make images and worship them.
>
> Do not use the name of the Lord your God in vain.
>
> Remember the Sabbath and keep it Holy.

Honor your mother and father that your days
may be long in the land I am giving you.

Do not kill.

Do not commit adultery.

Do not steal.

Do not bear false witness against your
neighbor.

Do not covet another's wife, slave, cattle,
donkey or anything else he owns.[4]

Theologians divide the commandments into two tables. The first table concerns the worship of God, God's name and God's day. The second table contains commandments that concern the nature of the Israelite community. This discussion begins with the second table because it specifically concerns the nature of Israel's alternative community.

It is often noted that, with the exception of the commandment, "Honor your mother and father," these commandments are all negative. They tell us what not to do. They say little if anything about what to do. We are commanded not to kill, but we are not told how to live with a person we do not kill. That seems to be left to our imagination. We are commanded to refrain from adultery. At the very least, this is a command to protect both one's own family and the family of others. This commandment gives us no idea of what a family is. (Today, a man living in a family like that of Jacob would be arrested.) We are commanded not to steal, but there is no guide concerning how we are to treat another person's property. There is not even a guide to what constitutes property. Many Native Americans, for example, did not believe it possible to own land. For them, the act of owning land was stealing.[5] We are commanded not to speak falsely about our neighbor. We are not told how to speak about our neighbor, nor are we told who our neighbor is. Finally, we are told not to covet. We are not told what our attitude toward the possessions of another ought to be. In short, the negative aspects of these commandments leave open a wide variety of possible actions. The community might find that it is important to create certain rules governing such behavior. This, however, means that such rules will always be contextual. That is to say, they exist because of the perceived needs of their

47

community of origin. They are not meant to be the rules that govern the life of all communities. They are not meant to be universal.

It must be remembered that the Commandments did not create Israel. God brought these 12 tribes into existence long before the commandments. Israel entered the Red Sea as Egyptian slaves. They emerged as a new socio-political reality that had to learn how to be an alternative to the dominant culture. The Commandments did not create Israel. They existed to protect Israel. They did not protect Israel from foreign invasion. They protected Israel from itself.[6] The Commandments marked the boundaries of this alternative community of Israel. That is to say, the alternative community of Israel would die if Israel routinely violated these commandments.

This is not exactly a threat. It is that not God was saying He would kill Israel if the Israelites violate the commandments. It is more a statement of the limits of the life of an alternative community. It is saying that if Israel, or perhaps any community, routinely disregards the commandments, it will not be an alternative to the dominant culture. The modern nation of Israel exists, but it is not the alternative community that God intended because its foreign and domestic policies routinely violate some of these commandments. Likewise, the United States exists, but it is not an alternative community because it routinely promotes coveting as the fuel for its economic system. God would not have killed Israel if Israel routinely violated the commandments. Israel would kill itself. Israel would cease to be an alternative community if murder becomes the norm rather than the terrible act it is. Israel would cease to be an alternative community if adultery, stealing, bearing false witness or coveting are norms instead of exceptions.

The commandment, "Honor your father and your mother that your days may be long in the land which the Lord your God gives you," (Ex. 20: 12) needs a little more discussion. First, it is important to note that this commandment does not say, "Obey your mother and father." It says, "Honor your mother and father." Parents of young children and adolescents have tried, mostly with great success, to substitute the word "obey" for the word "honor." The dominator system makes it in the interest of parents to make this substitution because it maintains the ranking of parents above children. If God issues a command to obey rather than honor one's parents, then everything a parent orders has divine support. It does not matter what mom and dad say. They must be obeyed. The substitution of the word obey for the word honor gives divine sanction both to the loving things parents do and to the violence and mental abuse parents sometimes inflict on their children. The substitution of "obey" for "honor" justifies the dominator system and the abuses that happen when ranking enters family life.

The words honor and obey are not the same. Honoring someone does not mean that you do exactly what that person says. Honoring someone means that you interpret his or her activities in the best way possible. This does not mean lying. It means that we honor our parents when we put the best possible "spin" on their actions and words.

The third thing to remember is that this and all the commandments are intended for adults, not children. It commands adults to honor their mothers and fathers. Moreover, the mothers and fathers to be honored probably should not be restricted to members of one's immediate family. Abraham and Sarah; Isaac and Rebecca; Jacob, Rachael and Leah; Ruth and Boaz; Moses and Zipporah; and Aaron and Miriam were the mothers and fathers of the 12 tribes of Israel. The 12 tribes of Israel were to honor these men and women. They were not to lie about the facts of their lives. They were to tell their stories in ways that gave honor to these mothers and fathers of Israel.

This commandment is the only one that has a promise associated with it. The promise says that, if the 12 tribes of Israel honor their mothers and fathers, they will live a long time in the land that God is giving them. Israel was, in fact, relatively successful in keeping this commandment. The Bible itself is testimony that they honored their mothers and fathers. The Bible tells stories of their mothers and fathers. It does not lie about these people. We see them "warts and all." Yet, the Bible interprets these people in relatively positive ways.

It is because Israel was faithful to this commandment that it distinguishes itself from all other people who walked away from the dominant culture. We continue to hear from the descendants of Israel. We no longer hear from the Olmec and the Hohokam. We do not know what happened to the Native Americans who walked away from their dominant cultures. We know more about the Israelites than any people who ever walked the face of the earth. We know of Israel because they honored their mothers and fathers. They continue to tell sagas of their parents, and they have kept themselves alive by telling these stories to this day. This is why they have survived the last 2,500 years without king, country or land. This is also why they are the most persecuted of all Western people; for, the dominator system recognizes the grave threat posed by people who walk away. This explains why the Jewish people are most threatened when the dominator system achieves its starkest manifestation. The Christians of medieval Europe terrorized the Jewish people whenever the dominator system – led by the Church – achieved most prominence. Stalinist Russia is another example, and Nazi Germany mounted the most systematic attempt to exterminate the Jews and was the place where the dominator system achieved its most blatant and insane form.

These descendants of the Exodus survived countless persecutions not because they used force to protect themselves. They survived because they honored their mothers and fathers. In honoring their parents, they kept their story alive. Their story begins when they walked away from their Egyptian captivity. It continues in their efforts to build a community that is an alternative to the dominant culture. Sometimes they are not faithful in their attempts. Sometimes they are. That they still live means they have been faithful enough. They are still a blessing to all nations because they still tell their story. They still honor their mothers and fathers.

There is one final and debatable question about the second table of commandments. Can they stand alone, or do they need divine support? Many people in contemporary society think that the second table can stand alone. In other words, they do not think that we need God to support not killing, not stealing, not committing adultery, not bearing false witness and not coveting. They think that these are self-evident truths and require no divine sanction. Others disagree. They believe that the second table needs divine sanction. Otherwise, the commands appear arbitrary. They are just a matter of opinion. They are not grounded in the nature of things. They are not the foundation of community.

Suffice it to say that the first table of the commandments held out hope to Israel. It helped them realize that they were not alone in their attempt to be an alternative community. While it is clear that alternative communities have been and can be developed apart from belief in Israel's God, it must be emphasized that Israel was very conscious of powerful opposition to its alternative experiment. Israel's God gave them hope when facing such opposition. It reminded the people of Israel that they are not left on their own in their efforts to form their alternative community. In this day and age, the dominator system is even more formidable. One need not be a believer to recognize the advantage the assistance of a God might bring in opposing the dominator system.

Laws Governing Israel's Internal Life

Great portions of Exodus, Leviticus, Numbers and Deuteronomy are devoted to the internal workings of the alternative community called Israel. These books contain laws concerning the treatment of strangers (Ex. 23: 9) and the treatment of slaves (Ex. 21: 1-11, Deut. 15: 12-18). There are numerous rules regarding offerings and sacrifices (Lev. 1-7, Numb. 15) and sexual purity (Deut. 21: 13-30, Lev. 18). Many regulations concerning religious festivals and holiness exist. There are dietary regulations (Lev. 11, Deut. 14: 3-21), rules concerning skin disease (Lev. 13:1-45; 14: 1-32) and even mildew control (Lev. 13: 46-59; Lev. 14: 33-53).

Today, few people even know these regulations. It is safe to say that not even the most avid fundamentalist Christian keeps them. Only the most Orthodox of the Jewish faith try to keep all these regulations. Few if any Christians, no matter how faithfully they think they keep to the strict letter of Scripture, would deem it necessary to purify a woman after childbirth according to the requirements of Leviticus 12. Only people who employ temporary workers even consider following Leviticus 19: 13 which says, "The wages of a hired servant shall not remain with you all night until morning." Only the Amish, Orthodox Jews and my son take Leviticus 19: 27 seriously. "You shall not round off the hair on your temples or mar the edges of your beard."

Israel had regulations we probably would consider evil. If a man marries a woman who he discovers is not a virgin, "then they shall bring out the young woman to the door of her father's house, and the men of her city shall stone her to death with stones"

(Deut. 22: 21). Anyone who does not keep the Sabbath, but works on that day is to be put to death (Ex. 31: 14). You should kill witches (Ex 22: 18). If parents have a rebellious son, they are to take him before the elders and accuse him of being disobedient and a drunkard. "Then all the men of the city shall stone him to death with stones; so you shall purge the evil from your midst; and all Israel shall hear and fear" (Deut. 21: 21). Finally, there is this rather odd rule. "When men fight with one another, and the wife of the one draws near to rescue her husband from the hand of him who is beating him, and puts out her hand and seizes him by the private parts, then you shall cut off her hand; your eye shall have no pity" (Deut. 25: 11). One wonders what set of circumstances could lead to the establishment of this rule.

These rules, along with dietary restrictions against eating shellfish (Lev. 11: 9,10; Deut 14: 9,10) and the regulations against wearing clothes made of two kinds of material (Lev. 19: 19), allow us to understand two things. First, very few people follow these rules anymore. Second, people are correct in not following all these rules because they were rules for the internal life of Israel. They are contextual. They are not meant to be absolute laws governing all human behavior.

All that was said about some of the strange internal laws of Israel should not detract from the fact that many of their rules might assist in the constitution of current alternative communities. For example, there are regulations against the mistreatment of strangers and foreigners that are derived from Israel's history. Of all people, Israel ought to remember what it is like to be a stranger in a strange land since they were strangers in Egypt (Ex. 22: 21; Ex. 23: 9; Lev. 19: 33, 34: Deut 27: 19). These laws are important because they are actually lessons in how diversity is to be treated in an alternative community. A stranger or foreigner is identifiable because he or she is different. Israel's internal regulations gave strangers and foreigners the rights of an Israelite (Lev. 19: 34). Such a regulation acknowledges the fact that foreigners have much to contribute to the life of Israel and that Israel is related to the world at large.

There are also regulations concerning the treatment of widows, orphans and the poor. (Ex.22: 22 – 24, 23: 6, 23: 11; Lev. 25: 1-7). Widows, orphans and the poor were marginalized by Israel's patriarchal social structure, which kept the dominator system alive in Israel and, as will be seen, contributed to Israel's official abandonment of its mission. Nonetheless, there are rules regarding the care and treatment of widows, orphans and poor within this terribly patriarchal society. While such laws may not be unprecedented in human history, they are essential to the creation of an alternative community. They remind the people that there are poor in their midst and that the poor are the culture's responsibility.

The very existence of a law that recognizes the rights of widows, orphans and the poor makes it more difficult to say that these people are morally responsible for their plight. These laws undermine the dominator system's control. Normally, those under the spell of the dominator system attempt to discover how the poor contributed to their own plight and thereby absolve the rich of their responsibility. Israel's regulations regarding the widow, orphan and poor do not allow us to distinguish between the morally "good" widows and the morally "bad" widows. Widows, orphans and poor have certain rights.

Israel also experimented with laws that denied the absolute power of the market place within its society. These laws are now called the Jubilee Code. They govern the Sabbath day, the Sabbath year and the Jubilee year. One theme of the Gospel of Luke is that Jesus was the fulfillment of the Jubilee Code.[7]

The Jubilee Code preserves the Sabbath day as a day of rest. On a superficial level, this means that no one is to work on the Sabbath no matter what the press of business might be. On a deeper level, this is the one day in the week that we do not act in accord with our own agenda, whatever that agenda might be. It is the day when we remember and appreciate life as the pure gift that it is.

The seventh year is the Sabbath year. The people of Israel can plant, harvest and gather for six years, but the seventh year is to be a year of "solemn rest for the land" (Lev. 25: 4). It is not clear if everyone observes the Sabbath year at the same time. The Sabbath year could have been a system of crop rotation whereby a farmer would not plant one seventh of his land each year. It is clear, however, that the Sabbath year had humanitarian as well as ecological purposes. During a Sabbath year, the owner of the land allows foreigners, slaves, hired men and domestic and wild animals to harvest whatever grew in uncultivated fields (Lev. 25: 6, 7).[8] The Sabbath year partially restores the sort of culture in existence before the agricultural revolution. In this year, food grows wild. Food is not a commodity. Food is not bought and sold. Food is not placed under "lock and key." On numerous occasions, Daniel Quinn states that the most fundamental characteristic of civilization is keeping our food under "lock and key." If this is true, then the Sabbath year negates this characteristic. Particularly if the Sabbath year was practiced on one seventh of the fields every year, this law assured that there would be "free food" for all of the people and animals in Israel.

The Sabbath year was also a time to cancel monetary debts (Deut. 15: 1-3). This code would shock most people steeped in capitalist ideology. Under capitalist ideology, the only reason to loan someone money is to make money. What reason could there possibly be to loan money to someone if one must forgive the debt in the Sabbath year? The only reason that I can think of is that the person is in need of the loan. A community that seeks to be an alternative to the dominator system might find this reason far more compelling than we do.

The seventh Sabbath year was the Jubilee year. This was the year that freedom was proclaimed to all the inhabitants of the land. "In this year all property that has been sold shall be restored to the original owner or his descendants" (Lev. 25: 10). This code prevented people from dealing unfairly with others (Lev. 25: 13). It recognized that possession is not 90% of the law. People impoverished by bad luck or the stupidity of previous generations will not be left without hope in Israel. The Jubilee year – the Year of Restoration – restores to their families what was sold or lost.

The Jubilee Code is so foreign to those under the spell of the dominator system that scholars have questioned whether the Israelites ever practiced such laws. Perhaps we can fathom the Sabbath year, but the Jubilee year seems unattainable by normal human beings. This attitude probably betrays our allegiance to the dominator system more than anything else. For a rather long period of time, Israel understood that its mission was to be different from other nations. The Jubilee Code is documentation of their attempt to be a community that was an alternative to the dominant culture.

Israel's Alternative Spirituality

The gods of the dominator system are unmoving and un-changing because they support a political order that is not supposed to change. The God of Israel is different. This God actually changes. This God makes adjustments. This God actually repents. Exodus 32: 7-14 is a dramatic illustration. Moses is on Mt. Sinai receiving the commandments from God. He has been gone a long time. The people below grow impatient. They demand that Aaron make them a god to lead them. Aaron complies. He gathers the jewelry from the people and quickly fashions a golden bull. Israel's God gets angry, and this conversation with Moses ensues:

> And the Lord said to Moses, "Go down; for your people whom you brought up out of the land of Egypt have corrupted themselves; they have turned aside quickly out of the way which I commanded them; they have made for themselves a molten calf, and have worshiped it and sacrificed to it, and said, 'These are your gods, O Israel, who brought you up out of the land of Egypt!'" And the Lord said to Moses, "I have seen this people, and behold,, it is a stiff-necked people; now therefore let me alone, that my wrath may burn hot against them and I may consume them; but of you I will make a great nation."
>
> But Moses besought the Lord his God, and said, "O Lord, why does thy wrath burn hot against thy people, whom thou hast brought forth out of the land of Egypt with great power and with a mighty hand? Why should the Egyptians say, 'With evil intent did He bring them forth, to slay them in the mountains, and to consume them from the face of the earth'? Turn from thy fierce wrath and repent of this evil against thy people. Remember Abraham, Isaac and Israel, thy servants, to whom thou dist swear by thine own self, and didst say to them 'I will multiply your descendants as stars of heaven, and all this land that I have promised I will give to your descendants, and they shall inherit it for ever.'" *And the Lord*

repented of the evil which he thought to do to his people. (Ex. 32: 7-14).

According to Brevard Childs, the key phrase in this text is God's request, "Now therefore, let me alone that my wrath may burn hot against them." This request assumes that God has made a decision. He has decided to destroy Israel. All God needs is Moses to leave Him alone. Had Moses thought that this God was like the gods of the dominator system, Moses would have had no recourse but to do as he was told. Gods of the dominator system do not change their minds. To change is to be defective, and the gods of the dominator system are not defective. To change is to be imperfect, and the gods of the dominator system are perfect. To change is to admit a limitation on power and knowledge, and the gods of the dominator system are omnipotent and omniscient. In short, if a god that supported the dominator system changed, that god would no longer be divine. The surprise is that Moses does not leave God alone. He does not obey God. Instead, Moses argues with God. In other words, Moses prays.[9]

Childs goes on to note that Moses makes three points in this prayer. First, he suggests that the newly emancipated slaves God now wishes to destroy are relatively new at being God's chosen people. Accordingly, God should make allowances. "O Lord, why does thy wrath burn hot against thy people, whom thou (just now) brought forth out of the land of Egypt?" Second, Moses argues that it would not be good public relations if God were to destroy Israel now. "Why should the Egyptians say, 'With evil intent did He bring them forth to slay them in the mountains, and to consume them from the face of the earth'?" Finally, Moses reminds God of the promises He made to Abraham, Isaac and Jacob.[10]

Moses' argument exhibits concern both for Israel's future and for God's future.[11] He realizes that a new thing is being done with this group of emancipated slaves. He recognizes that the Israelites only know life under the dominator system and their adjustment to this new way will take time. Thus, Moses reminds God that this new community requires patience if it is to come to fruition. Moses is concerned about God as well. This may sound strange to our ears, but this is because our understanding of God is greatly influenced by the dominator system. As has been suggested, gods of the dominator system are perfect and unchanging. They do not need "suggestions" on how they should act. When Moses refuses to leave God alone so His wrath may burn hot against the Israelites, Moses recognized that this God was not a god of the dominator system. This God supported a partnership way. Just as Israel was new at being God's chosen people, their God was new at being Israel's God. This God had not intervened in history before the Exodus. Intervention was not necessary when humanity lived in accord with partnership ways, but now God had to intervene on behalf of partnership ways. The emergence of the dominator system had forced God's hand. Even God was not too clear about what must be done. Moreover, if this text is to be believed, the God of Israel now is tempted to adopt the way of the dominator system. As the Pharaoh had once tried to kill Israel, the "God of Israel" now wants to kill them.

Moses convinces the God of Israel to *repent of the evil he was about to do to Israel*. In this crucial instance, God turns his back on the ways of the dominator system once and for all. Israel's God is not so sure of what the future brings. Israel's God does not seem to be in complete control, but through Moses and Israel, this God is beginning to understand what a partnership life means. God will resist the dominator system without using the destructive techniques of the dominator system.

A new spirituality emerges in Moses' dialogue with God. The gods of the dominator system could not change because the dominator system allows but one way to live. In the ancient world, this way consisted of religious and political leaders at the top. These people were supported by a larger military group. The vast majority of people lived in poverty. The gods of such systems upheld this order. They could not change. Change undermined the social order. If God could change, then the social order could change. This would give hope to those oppressed by the social order and be a cause for grave concern for those whose riches depended on the "unchanging" established order.

The God of Israel not only changes as a consequence of this dialogue with Moses, *God repents of the evil he planned to do to Israel.* The Exodus event revealed that the God of Israel could change the political order. This dialogue with Moses disclosed that this God did not emancipate Israel in order to place them into another unchanging political order. This God changed His mind! This God repented! This God did these things as a consequence of an ongoing dialogue with the people! Thus, any social order could be altered by men and women engaged in conversation with God.

The books of Exodus, Leviticus, Numbers and Deuteronomy concern the creation of a new social entity. This new group attempts to be an alternative to civilizations that were under the spell of the dominator model. The Israelites realized that the monarchies of the dominator system were inconsistent with the society they wanted to form. Hence, they became a loose confederation of tribes ruled by judges.

Israel recognized that, like all communities, this alternative community needs boundaries. The Ten Commandments established these boundaries by revealing behavior that, if routinely practiced, would undermine the alternative community and re-establish the dominator system. These commandments did not designate the actual behavior required within such a community. They only established the ethical limits of the alternative community. The people of Israel did, however, address issues of how *they* should live in *their own* version of an alternative community. In other words, most of the rules delineated in Exodus, Leviticus, Numbers and Deuteronomy are not meant to be absolutes that govern the moral practices of all human beings. They are rules for *Israel's* social life. These are uncomfortable words for people who like to think that each rule in the Bible is true for all time, but we have seen that few people even attempt to follow all of Israel's laws. If you have eaten shellfish or a cheeseburger, you have not obeyed Israel's dietary restrictions.

The fact that we do not follow many of the rules governing the internal life of Israel is not a bad thing. There are many ways to be an alternative to the dominant culture. Israel was trying its own way. The Torah records their attempt.

Finally, Israel developed a different spirituality. Their spirituality did not merely confirm the established order as the religious practices of the dominator system do. Their spirituality was grounded in conversations with God (prayer). They believed that prayer could even change God's mind. This meant that all parties to the conversation made adjustments on the basis of the conversation. Even God made adjustments, and this possibility gave people hope in situations that would have been thought hopeless under the dominator system.

It must be understood that all efforts to establish an alternative to the dominator system can be co-opted by the dominator system itself. If, for example, a king displaces the system of judges, then prayer rapidly becomes the exclusive domain of the monarchy. This, in fact, occurred in Israel. When Israel became a monarchy, it officially abandoned its partnership way and accepted the dominator system. This acceptance was never, however, complete, but the dominator system became an important feature of Israel's life until the present.

Chapter 4:

The Collapse of the Mosaic Alternative

It is not fair to say that Israel was a failure in its struggle to be an alternative to the dominator system. Israel was unlike other nations for almost 250 years. Whereas other nations were monarchies ruled by kings and Pharaohs, Israel was a loose confederation of 12 tribes organized around judges. Even when Israel anointed a king, prophets emerged in opposition to the monarchy's claims of absolute power. Prophets always reminded those who would listen that there was an alternative to the dominant culture. Even when Israel was conquered by other nations, these prophets reminded Israel that God still offered an alternative to their plight. Because they somehow have kept this vision alive, the landless descendants of Jacob have been a thorn in the side of all cultures under the control of the dominator system for over 2,500 years. This is the real reason they have been persecuted and oppressed by adherents of the dominator system.

The Emergence of Israel's Monarchy

The fact remains, however, that the people of Israel grew tired of being governed differently from other nations. Accordingly, the people approached Samuel, Israel's high priest and the last of the judges, and asked him to anoint a king over them. As the story goes, Samuel was reluctant to do this because he, in accord with the 250 years of rule by judges, believed that God was the King of Israel. To place a human being on the throne of Israel was to deny the rule of God.

Samuel prayed. God told him to listen to the voice of the people and that the people have not rejected him, they have rejected God as their king (I Sam. 8: 4-9). God did, however, tell Samuel to warn the people of Israel about having a king, and to do so with these words.

These will be the ways of the king who will
reign over you: he will take your sons and appoint

them to his chariots and to be his horsemen, and to run before his chariots; and he will appoint for himself commanders of thousands and commanders of fifties, and some to plow his ground and to reap his harvest, and to make his implements of war and the equipment of his chariots. He will take your daughters to be perfumers and cooks and bakers. He will take the best of your fields and vineyards and olive orchards and give them to his servants. He will take the tenth of your grain and of your vineyards and give it to his officers and to his servants. He will take your menservants and maidservants, and the best of your cattle and your asses, and put them to his work. He will take the tenth of your flocks, and you shall be his slaves. And in that day you will cry out because of your king, whom you have chosen for yourselves; but the lord will not answer you in that day." (I Sam. 8: 10-18.)

Despite such warnings, the people were determined to be like other nations. They desired to have a king. The allures of the dominator system were too great.

The movement from a confederation of tribes to monarchy began "a process of rapid erosion of the basic principles of the new religious ethic that stems from Moses."[1] This erosion is expressed subtly at first. It can be seen in Israel's first king Saul who was obsessed with prestige. During the period of the Judges, Israel believed God alone led Israel into battle. Certain people like Gideon (Judges 6, 7, 8) or Deborah (Judges 4) would be raised up to lead Israel, but it was always understood that God was the actual leader. There was no glory for the general. The victory belonged to God.

Saul's obsession with prestige indicates a shift in Israel's attitude toward warfare. War now enhanced the prestige and fame of the military leader. It provided booty for the soldiers. Moreover, the people of Israel promoted this ideological shift. After David killed Goliath, for example, there was a great celebration. Young women from every town ran to meet Saul and his army. They sang, "Saul killed thousands, and David tens of thousands," and Saul grew jealous of David (I Sam. 18: 7). This passage reveals that Saul was concerned with power and prestige and that the people were placing their faith in their warriors instead of God.

> . . . it was the adolescent adulation of young girls in Judea that not only caused David's rise to fame, but also illustrated the radical changes in the ideology of ancient Israelites. The glorification of Yahweh as the 'divine warrior' who led his people to victory over the kings in the old poetry of the Federation period has now given way to the glorification of the professional warrior for his superior ability to commit murder. The old 'heroic' mentality that regarded military successes as a major theme of epic chant returns with a vengeance very soon after the reversion to Bronze Age political organization in Israel. Yahweh was not nearly so reliable a source of 'security' as an effective military general.[2]

The Mosaic experiment continued to collapse under King David. David conquered Jerusalem which became his capital. Its bureaucracy was assimilated, and bureaucratic rule became the norm. Harems were established. Foreign treaties were developed. Trade increased. Prosperity abounded. The paganization of government led to an entirely new cultic life that bore little relationship to the worship life of the former confederacy.[3]

By the time of Solomon, Israel had thoroughly abandoned Moses' and Jethro's social vision. In place of the system of tribes, Solomon instituted a system of administrative districts. This elaborate bureaucracy institutionalized conservative reasoning practices that eliminated most issues of justice and compassion. Wisdom was emphasized. Royal propaganda said that King Solomon was the wisest king alive. Wisdom literature was developed. Wisdom was an effort to manage reality and undermine alternatives to the monarch's understanding of life.[4] Only the experts, after all, were wise. As a consequence, only the judgment of the experts was trusted by the populace. The monarchy convinced the people that it had the monopoly on wisdom. Finally, a standing army was instituted. It allowed the king to wage war at his whim rather than rely on the agreement of the people (or the rush of God's Spirit).

Solomon's reversal of Israel's alternative community was characterized by three elements. First, Solomon's kingdom was very rich (I Kings 4: 20). Indeed, affluence is the key to understanding Solomon's power. Since most human beings desire to have their stomach's filled, most will submit to most any kind of indignity if the source of the indignity is also the source of food.[5] Like most leaders within the dominator system, King Solomon used his control of food to control his followers.

Second, Solomon oppressed those he could not control with his riches. The Bible itself indicates that social oppression was one source of Solomon's wealth. A small percentage of people lived extremely well off of the work of the many. A larger, but still small percentage lived pretty well by keeping the vast majority of people in their place. This social structure continues to be the most ubiquitous economic characteristic of cultures that serve the dominator system. Solomon's regime was not an exception. It controlled the energy and the resources of the many so that the opulence of Solomon's court could be maintained (I Kings 5: 13-18, 9: 22). Solomon even used the forced labor of the Israelites themselves. When he built the Temple, it is said that he forced 30,000 men to work on the project (I Kings 5: 13).

Finally, Solomon reversed Moses' spiritual revolution. Not only did Solomon's Temple project make slaves of the very people that God had liberated from Egypt, the theology of the Temple reversed the spiritual revolution begun by Moses. Mosaic spirituality was democratic. All people had access to God through prayer and ritual. The Temple was a visible reminder to the people of Israel that God was now thoroughly connected to the court of Solomon. It gave the king direct access to God while it denied the people such access. From the moment the Temple was built, news from God came filtered through the king and his priests.

> God is now on call, and access to him is con-
> trolled by the royal court. Such an arrangement
> serves two interlocking functions. On the one
> hand, it assures ready sanction to every notion of
> the king because there can be no transcendent re-
> sistance or protest. On the other hand, it gives the
> king a monopoly so that no marginal person may
> approach God except on the king's own terms.

There will be no disturbing cry against the king here.[6]

Solomon countered the counter-culture of Moses. He traded the economics of equality (as reflected in the Jubilee Code and laws upholding the rights of widows, orphans, foreigners and the poor) for an economics of affluence that routinely disregarded and oppressed the marginalized. Solomon substituted a politics of oppression for a politics of justice, and, in order that these economic and political changes might appear sanctioned by God, Solomon built the Temple to be the religious center of his empire.[7] The irony is that Solomon still called his God by the same name Moses used. Moses' God was the one who had liberated 12 Hebrew tribes from their slavery under the Egyptian dominator system. Solomon used the name of his new God to keep people within his dominator system. Under the Mosaic scheme, people had more direct access to God through the many judges in Israel. Solomon was able to deny this access, and restrict it to kings and their court priests. Everything was reversed. It was as if Israel had never been liberated from Egypt.

Voices of Opposition

In 931 BC, Solomon died and his kingdom was divided. The Northern Kingdom called Israel was composed of 10 tribes and the Southern Kingdom of Judah consisted of 2 tribes. The dominator system persisted in the Northern Kingdom of Israel until 722 BC when the Kingdom of Israel was conquered by Assyria. Its population was dispersed throughout the Middle East. These tribes are lost to history. The dominator system managed to survive in the Kingdom of Judah until 587 BC when Judah was conquered by the Babylonians. The people of Judah (hereafter called Jews because of the name of this kingdom) were also exiled. These people were not lost. After two generations, some returned to their homeland. Persia conquered the once invincible Babylonia, and the Persian King Cyrus allowed the exiles who so desired to return to Jerusalem.

The dominator system appears to have prevailed in Israel after Solomon. It was the way the kings of the Northern Kingdom of Israel ruled. It was how the kings of Judah governed as well. It also prevailed when Israel and Judah were defeated by foreign powers; for, Israel and Judah fell to empires under the sway of the dominator system. Nevertheless, the dominator system never held a total monopoly in and among the people of Israel. Someone always spoke against the official policies of the monarchies. Amos and Hosea did so in the Northern Kingdom of Israel. Jeremiah and Ezekiel did the same in Judah. The one we now call second Isaiah allowed the Jews in Babylonian captivity to imagine alternatives to even the mighty Babylon. The prophet Daniel even opposed the Persian version of the dominator system.

The prophet Amos (c. 780-742 BC) challenged the economics of affluence and the politics of oppression that Solomon had established and that the Northern Kingdom of Israel had continued. Under the dominator system, affluence usually has some theological or ideological justification, and Israel was not an exception. The religious leaders developed an ideology that asserted that Israel's affluence was a consequence of divine favor. This is a very convenient ideology for the rich because it justifies them and absolves them of their responsibility to the poor.

The prophet Amos shattered this ideology. Possibly for the first time in human history, the prophet Amos exposed relationship between affluence and oppression. "They sell the righteous for silver, and the needy for a pair of shoes – they that trample the head of the poor into the dust of the earth, and turn aside the way of the afflicted" (Amos 2: 6, 7). To make matters worse, Amos realized that those under the grip of the dominator system do not even know how to be honest. They store up their goods, and they do so through crime and violence. They do not even know they are doing these things (Amos 3: 10).

Amos thought that the people did not even know they were acting unjustly because they had devised a religious system that masks their injustice even from themselves. In the Mosaic experiment, it was clear that the alternative community required justice and compassion for the poor. The Northern Kingdom of Israel seemed to believe that God desired only the ritualistic sacrifices of the rich. Once the proper sacrifice was made, the rich person could go out and plunder the poor. The success of the Temple ideology was that it eliminated questions of justice and replaced them with questions of cultic obligation. This led people to believe that their obligations to justice could be met through sacrificial worship. The poor could now be neglected because all obligations to justice had been met through the Temple cult. It is because the God of Moses desires political and economic justice and because their sacrifices prevented the people from acting justly that Amos wrote,

> The Lord says, "I hate, I despise your feasts, and I take no delight in your solemn assemblies. Even though you offer me your burnt offerings and cereal offerings, I will not accept them, and the peace offerings of your fatted beasts, I will not look upon. Take away from me the noise of your songs; to the melody of your harps I will not listen. But let justice roll down like waters and righteousness like an ever-flowing stream." (Amos 5: 21-24).

Israel had succumbed to the dominator system. Amos believed the consequence of this was destruction.

Apparently, Amos thought destruction was an inevitable fact for all nations that fell under the dominator system's spell. The book of Amos begins with a litany of the sins of other nations that will most certainly lead to their punishment and destruction (Amos 1: 3 - 2: 5). Israel's fate will be like the fate of these nations because Israel has also subjected itself to the same forces that led to the destruction of all nations – their preference for the dominator system.

> Woe to those who are at ease in Zion, and to those who feel secure on the mountain of Samaria.... Pass over to Calneh, and see; and thence go to Hamath the great; then go down to Gath of the Philistines. Are they better than these kingdoms? Or is their territory greater than your territory, O you who put far away the evil day, and bring near the seat of violence... I abhor the pride of Jacob and hate his strongholds; and I will deliver up the city and all that is in it (Amos 6: 1-2, 8).

Amos' message was that the Northern Kingdom of Israel would be destroyed because it had been unfaithful to its origins. It had been created to be an alternative to the dominator system, but it had failed this mission. It had become just like other nations.

Israel would be destroyed because it had conformed to the dictates of the dominator system. Now, the Bible's theology demands that this destruction be at the hands of God. As was true with the Pharaoh's hard heart, however, a more secular explanation is possible. Like all empires, Israel crumbled because of the weight of the dominator system. Events simply took their "natural" course, and the "natural course" for all societies under the spell of the dominator system is destruction and death. The book of Amos tells us this in the first two chapters where it speaks of the demise of many nations known to Israel. Like Israel, their crimes were their preference for an economics of affluence over an economics of equality, a politics of oppression over a politics of justice and a religion exclusive to the monarchy over a religion where the people had access to God. It is Amos' contention that these practices lead to destruction of the social order.

Do not falsely conclude that Amos' warnings apply only to ancient civilizations. Remember the Soviet Union. That near invincible power just stopped. One fine day near the end of the 20th century, the Soviet Union collapsed. No shots were fired. It collapsed because the great powers of the dominator system always collapse when left to their own devices.

Over a century after Amos and the demise of the Northern Kingdom of Israel, the Southern Kingdom of Judah was on the verge of being conquered by the Babylonian Empire. Like their relatives in the Northern Kingdom of Israel, the people of Judah were complacent. They simply went on doing what they were doing. They appeared oblivious to their fate.

They rationalized their complacency with an ideology that taught that Judah would not be conquered because Judah had the Temple of the Lord. The official propaganda was that God lived in Jerusalem. God's home was the Temple that Solomon had built. Nothing, not even a great Empire, could prevail against God's Temple. Judah was safe.

The prophet Jeremiah countered this ideology. Speaking only the words God had told him to speak, Jeremiah warned Judah:

> Thus says the Lord of hosts, the God of Israel,
> "Amend your ways and your doings, and I will let
> you dwell in this place. Do not trust in these de-

ceptive words: 'This is the temple of the Lord, the temple of the Lord, the temple of the Lord.'"

"For if you truly amend your ways and your doings, if you truly execute justice one with another, if you do not oppress the alien, the fatherless or the widow, or shed innocent blood in this place, and if you do not go after other gods to your own hurt, then I will let you dwell in this place, in the land that I gave of old to your fathers forever."

"Behold, you trust in deceptive words to no avail. Will you steal, murder, commit adultery, swear falsely, burn incense to Ba'al, and go after other gods that you have not known, and then come and stand before me in this house, which is called by my name, and say, 'We are delivered!' only to go on doing all these abominations? Has this house, which is called by my name, become a den of robbers in your eyes? Behold, I myself have seen it, says the Lord. Go now to my place that was in Shiloh, where I made my name dwell at first, and see what I did to it for the wickedness of my people Israel. And now, because you have done all these things, says the Lord, and when I spoke to you persistently you did not answer, therefore I will do to the house which is called by my name, and in which you trust, and to the place which I gave to you and to your fathers, as I did to Shiloh, and I will cast you out of my sight, as I cast out all your kinsmen, all the offspring of Ephraim." (Jr. 7: 3 - 15).

This speech is quoted at length because it is a specific attack on the religious ideology of Solomon as well as a general attack on the religious ideologies of the dominator system.

Every dominator system uses religion to bolster the imperial agenda. Solomon used religion for his imperial purposes when he built the Temple. In this process, he placed God at the call of the king and gave the king a monopoly on access to God. This enabled Solomon and the kings who followed him to create religious ideologies that gave divine sanction to the political agenda of the monarchy. In the case of Judah's monarchy, this ideology came to include the idea that the Temple of the Lord guaranteed the safety of the people of Judah – particularly the leadership of the people of Judah. That the prophet Jeremiah understood this to be royal propaganda is demonstrated by the repetition of this ideology as if it were a jingle in a modern television commercial. "Do not trust these deceptive words, 'This is the temple of the Lord, The temple of the Lord, The temple of the Lord.'" (Jr. 7: 4).

It was Adolph Hitler's propaganda minister Goebbels who said that you can get people to believe almost anything if you simply repeat it often enough. It seems the kings Josiah (640-609 BC), Jehoiakim (609-598 BC) and Zedekiah (598-587 BC) knew this fact long before this evil man articulated it. Apparently, they thought that if they merely repeated their slogan, "The Temple of the Lord," often enough, people would come to believe that the monarchy and Judah were safe simply because of the existence of a particular building.

The "Temple of the Lord" ideology also generated complacency in Judah's foreign and domestic policy. The idea that Judah's foes could not conquer her because of the presence of the Temple of the Lord led Judah to disregard the Babylonian threat. More importantly, however, the "Temple of the Lord" ideology allowed the rulers and the affluent to disregard the plight of the marginalized. This was in direct opposition to the social system that Moses and his followers had established. Jeremiah mentions this. He begins saying that Judah will be spared if they stop doing what they are doing and stop oppressing the widow, orphan and foreigner (the very people that the Torah's Jubilee Code protected). They are to obey the Commandments and refrain from stealing, murdering, adultery, and slander. Finally, they are not to believe the royal ideology that tells them that all will be well because they have the Temple of the Lord (Jr. 7: 5 – 7).

Jeremiah 7: 3 – 15 then draws a connection between the deceptive royal ideology and the practice of social and economic exploitation. Those who proclaim this deceptive ideology the loudest are the same people who practice these social abominations. The royal ideology enables them to do this because it makes the Temple of the Lord a safe haven for robbers. As long as these people have the Temple of the Lord, they think they are safe. Since they think they are safe, they believe they can oppress the foreigner, widow and orphan, disregard the God's Commandments and still survive as God's people. The royal monopoly on God enables these injustices to prevail.

Jeremiah's final assault on Solomon's dominator regime is the prediction that this entire system will collapse. Like Amos, Jeremiah believes that this collapse is not the result of Judah being conquered by a stronger power. Jeremiah believed that Judah would fall because it lost divine support. Judah lost God's support for one reason. It abandoned the Mosaic attempt to be an alternative to the dominator system. It tried to be like other nations, and it became indistinguishable from all nations under the dominator system. In 587 BC, the Babylonians conquered Judah, exiled the people and destroyed the Temple of the Lord.

The demise of Judah should have been the end of the Mosaic attempt to create a community that was an alternative to the dominant culture, but it was not. Unlike the 10 tribes of Israel who were conquered and scattered by Assyria in 722 BC, the descendants of the two tribes of Judah are still with us. They remain largely because of the voices of the same prophets who predicted Judah's destruction, namely Jeremiah and Ezekiel. Jeremiah and Ezekiel were men of different temperaments. Jeremiah was greatly distressed by his God-given mission. He cursed the day he was born because of the message he had to say to Judah (Jr. 15: 10). He took no delight in the demise of his beloved Jerusalem. He truly wished that things could have been otherwise. Ezekiel, on the other hand, did not seem to mind too much. He appeared quite willing to speak God's Word to Jerusalem and let the chips fall where they may.

This being said, the messages of Ezekiel and Jeremiah were very similar in two fundamental respects. Prior to the fall of Judah, Jeremiah and Ezekiel offered no hope to Judah apart from Judah's repentance. Ironically, the people of Judah were quite hopeful at this time. Their "Temple of the Lord" ideology gave them this hope, and they saw no need to repent. After the fall of Jerusalem, the people lost all hope. Their ideology of the Temple failed them. They marched off into exile. It was only at this time that Jeremiah and Ezekiel offered their words of hope.

These prophets had a different source of hope than that of those against whom they had prophesied. The leadership of Judah – the dominator system's well fed ten percent – placed their hope in the trappings of the dominator system. Moreover, these leaders also controlled the minds and hearts of the general population through their "Temple of the Lord" propaganda. Thus, all of Judah lost hope when Jerusalem fell to the Babylonians and the Temple was destroyed.

Jeremiah and Ezekiel did not place their hope in the trappings of the dominator system. They placed their hope in the God of Moses and in the alternative community they believed their God was trying to create. To demonstrate his belief that hope was not dead, Jeremiah purchased a field from his cousin Hanamel only months before Jeremiah's predicted fall of Jerusalem (Jr. 32: 1-15). This demonstrated his belief that the exile would not be permanent and that he or his descendants would return to get the land.

Ezekiel demonstrated the source of his hope in the narration of his vision of a valley full of dry bones (Ez. 37: 1-14). Upon seeing this vision, Ezekiel is asked if these dead, dry bones can live. He replies that only God knows. He is told to prophesy to the bones and Ezekiel does so. Suddenly, there was a great rattling sound as the bones came together. Muscle tissue developed on the bones. Flesh covered them, but there was no life in them. Then Ezekiel was told to prophesy to the wind. (In Hebrew the word for wind, breath and Spirit is the same). The breath of life came, and the field of dry bones sprung back to life. Finally, Ezekiel's strange vision receives an interpretation. God told Ezekiel that these dead, dry bones represent the whole house of Israel. After its defeat by the Babylonians, Israel thinks it is dead. It has lost all hope. It has been cut off completely. God then tells Ezekiel to prophesy to this hopeless people saying:

> And you shall know that I am the Lord, when I open your graves, and raise you from your graves, O my people. And I will put my Spirit within you, and you shall live, and I will place you in your own land; then you shall know that I, the Lord, have spoken, and I have done it, says the Lord (Ez. 37:13, 14).

Like Jeremiah, Ezekiel narrates this vision of hope only after the fall of Jerusalem. Only after the previous source of Judah's hope was destroyed does Ezekiel offer a word of hope. Only now could they understand that God, rather than the dominator system, was the source of hope.

The very structure of the book of Ezekiel demonstrates the contention that hope is not offered until the source of Judah's false hope was destroyed. The first 24 chapters happen in pre-exilic times. Here Ezekiel offers only a massive critique of pre-exilic Judah. There is no hope offered apart from Judah's repentance in this section. There are only announcements of Jerusalem's impending doom. The second part of Ezekiel is more hopeful, but it begins after Jerusalem has fallen. It is only at this point that Ezekiel offers hope.[8]

Hope must wait until Jerusalem's fall because hopeful words are always misconstrued by those in the grip of the dominator system. If a word of hope is spoken to a person in the clutches of the dominator system, that word will quickly be used to reinforce the powers of the dominator system itself. For example, if a New York City stockbroker hears a message of hope, it is likely that he or she will think the message pertains to the stock market increasing its value. If a word of hope is given to a Democrat, he or she will associate it with a victory by the Democratic Party. Likewise, if Ezekiel had given a word of hope to the King of Judah, then that word would have been interpreted as victory over Babylonia.

In waiting until the fall of Jerusalem to offer a word of hope, Ezekiel waited for the demise of the false objects of hope that his contemporaries had relied upon. Hope was no longer found in the Solomonic way. That way had been overthrown. Hope could only be found in the One who had liberated the Israelites from the Egyptians. Perhaps, the God of Moses would do this again. Perhaps those exiled in Babylon would be rescued once more. That was the hope that both Ezekiel and Jeremiah offered. It would not, however, happen overnight. The people of Judah were exiled in Babylon.

Prophetic Voices from Babylonian Exile

The temptations the exiles encountered in Babylonia were similar to those to which they succumbed in Judah. Just as Solomon and his successors abandoned Mosaic reforms and adopted the dominator system, those in exile were tempted to forget Mosaic reforms and adopt the Babylonia version of the dominator system.[9] Like all cultures in the clutches of the dominator system, it was the Babylonian agenda to destroy all alternatives to its rule. These alternatives included foreign as well as domestic threats. Ideas were just as threatening as military maneuvers.

It is into this situation that the author of Isaiah 40-56 writes. Often called Second Isaiah, this unnamed prophet speaks the unthinkable. The prophet speaks words of comfort to people who have lost homeland, religion and autonomy. The prophet speaks of returning home to exiles who were trying to make the best of their situation by adopting Babylonian ways. The prophet proclaims a new world order to people tempted to accept Babylon's vision of reality as the only possible definition of life.[10] Second Isaiah offers a word of comfort and hope to people who have no reason to hope if they live by the standards of the dominator system.

Second Isaiah begins with these comforting words. "Comfort, Comfort my people, says your God. Speak tenderly to Jerusalem, and cry to her that her warfare is ended, that her iniquity is pardoned, that she has received from the Lord's hand double for all her sins" (Is. 40: 1, 2). Today we mistakenly believe that poetry like that of Second Isaiah is innocuous, but this is a severe underestimation. These alternative visions occasionally change the world. Isaiah's poetry gives the exiles an alternative to Babylon's view of reality. Isaiah's poetry is not a dream. It has a chance of becoming reality. Political events are cited which, if interpreted in accord with Isaiah's vision, lead his listeners to suspect that the hope that was being offered had support in the political reality of the day (Is. 45). Isaiah's alternative vision allowed the exiles to see Persia differently. Instead of being just another empire, Second Isaiah understood the empire of Persia to be the agent of Israel's return. Second Isaiah even understood Cyrus, the Persian king, to be anointed by God for the purpose of restoring the exiles to their homeland. He would defeat Babylonia and allow the exiles to go home. Most certainly Cyrus did not interpret his rule in this manner, but, if Cyrus is remembered at all in this day and age, he is remembered as much for allowing the exiles to return to Jerusalem as anything else.

Once again, it is the context that differentiates Second Isaiah from Ezekiel and Jeremiah. These prophets spoke different words because they were in different contexts. They all challenged the dominator system. Jeremiah and Ezekiel spoke against the dominator system as it was expressed in Judah. Their words were words of judgment and defeat for Judah. Isaiah challenged the Babylonian expression of the dominator system. This challenge was one of hope for the exiles and one of destruction for the Babylonian Empire. All the prophets expressed alternatives to the dominator system. Where the dominator system tried to convince people that its view of reality was the only possible way to live, the prophets created and recalled alternative ways. Where the dominator system claimed that national security was the ultimate value, the prophets spoke words of justice for widows, orphans and foreigners. Where the leadership in the dominator system claimed a monopoly on access to the divine, the prophets, by their very existence, indicated that access to God was far more democratic.

One should never forget that the words of the prophets are sounded at particular times and in particular places. In other words, they are contextual. The same word in a different context alters the meaning and significance of the word. We have already noted that Second Isaiah begins with words of comfort (Is. 40:1). These words are spoken to people in exile who, by the standards of the dominator system, have no reason to be comfortable. If these words apply to us at all, it is because our context is similar to the context in which these words were first expressed. If suburban Americans can be thought of as exiles, and some think they can, then perhaps these words of comfort apply. More likely, however, suburban Americans are like those in ancient Judah who clung to their ideology and riches until their culture came to an abrupt end. If this is so, the words of pre-exilic Jeremiah and Ezekiel are far more applicable.

Surprisingly, this emphasis on context brings us to a discussion of the first chapter of Genesis. This is an important text to discuss at this time because Genesis 1 was actually written during or immediately after the exilic period. It certainly achieved its final form immediately after the exile. Accordingly, it is an effort by a recently liberated people to distinguish themselves from their former captors. When we interpret this marvelous piece of literature, we generally disregard this context. We make the mistake of placing this poetry directly into our context and act as if it is some kind of Biblical broadside against modern theories of evolution and genetics. This poetic account of creation could not have been written against modern scientific theories for the simple reason that its author(s) did not know such theories.

What the author(s) did know, however, is very interesting. They did know a variety of creation myths. In particular, they knew the creation myths of their Babylonian captors. This is the forgotten context of this creation story.

Nearly every creation story in the environs of ancient Israel said that creation was a violent act. Someone or more likely some god was slaughtered by another god, and the cosmos came into existence because of this violent act. Walter Wink calls this belief that violence both restores and establishes life "the myth of redemptive violence."[11] Wink is wise enough to recognize that the myth of redemptive violence is not limited to the ancient world. He maintains that it is the dominant myth of an American culture that is convinced that war is the way to peace, and military strength guarantees security.[12] It may well be that the myth of redemptive violence is a myth fundamental to the dominator system.

The first chapter of Genesis was written in opposition to the myths of redemptive violence in general, and the Babylonian creation myth in particular. The Babylonian creation myth has a standard format. The goddess Tiamat has a number of offspring. These "younger" gods upset the "older" gods because of their constant noise. (Apparently, peace and quiet is the first casualty of parenthood for gods as well as humans). The "older" gods adopt a radical solution to their problem. They decide to kill their offspring to restore tranquility. The "younger" deities hear of the plot, and the youngest of all, Marduk, volunteers to kill Tiamat before she can kill them. Marduk is not, however, an altruist. He wants to be rewarded for his services. Before undertaking his mission, Marduk gets his siblings to grant him supremacy if he is successful. After receiving such assurances, Marduk slays Tiamat.

Marduk forms the cosmos out of her body and places Babylon at the center of the cosmos. Human beings are created to serve the gods. The cosmos, Babylonia and the human race all owe their existence to this violent primordial act of creation.

The story does not end here. Tiamat does not exactly stay dead. How could she? She is a god! Each year, her anti-cosmic life force attempts to reassert itself. The growing season ends. Plants die. The Babylonian civilization as well as life itself appears to be endangered by the potential lack of food. The people begin to worry that this annual "winter" season will be permanent. Something must be done! Babylonia's only recourse was to try to revive Marduk. Apparently he was sleeping or lost interest in the cosmos. So, each year the Babylonian people had a five-day religious festival designed to "revive" Marduk and urge him to slay the rebellious Tiamat once again. To this end, religious ritual repeated the violent act of creation, and the natural order was restored. These rituals were the center of Babylon's economic and religious life.

Lest we wonder how these poor, misguided Babylonians could perpetuate such a blatant untruth, we must consider this. Each year on the day after Thanksgiving, contemporary Americans begin a buying frenzy that mimics the Babylonian revival of Marduk. Rotund men in red suites and long white beards appear in shopping centers. People cram into the parking lots of these shopping centers for the privilege of standing in long lines to buy unnecessary items. All the while, religious music is being piped into the stores. The only difference between our buying frenzy and the Babylonian religious frenzy is our practice lasts a month. Their ritual lasted only five days.

Some might say that the difference between the Babylonian ritual and ours is greater than the duration of the event. After all, the Babylonians were performing a *religious* ritual. They were trying to revive their God. This difference, however, is not as clear-cut as it might appear to be. Throughout the period of our buying frenzy, people we call economists are interviewed by journalists and televisions personalities. The question they most often ask is, "Will all the buying during the holiday (a word derived from Holy day) season be enough to *revive* the Economy?" It probably is not too much of an exaggeration to say that if our culture has a god at all its name is "the Economy!" If so, our efforts to revive "the Economy" cannot be too far removed from Babylonia's efforts to revive Marduk.

Walter Wink contends that our relationship to the Babylonian creation myth may even be closer than this. He asserts that, like the Babylonians, we may still be under the influence of the myth of redemptive violence.[13] Wink demonstrates that the cartoons our children watch, the movies adults see and the foreign policy our nation conducts all assume the truth of the myth of redemptive violence. In an analysis that would be quite amusing if it were not so profoundly true, Wink uses "Popeye" cartoons as an example of the myth of redemptive violence in children's television. All "Popeye" cartoons begin with Popeye peacefully courting his beautiful girl friend Olive Oyle. A violent man named Bluto (in the older cartoons) and Brutus (in the new cartoons) violates this tranquility. He beats Popeye to a pulp and sexually assaults Olive Oyle. After getting beaten within inches of death, Popeye eats spinach. This gives him godlike strength with which he proceeds to kick Bluto's butt. This act of redemptive violence restores the original harmony in much the same way as the revived Marduk restored harmony by subduing Tiamat in Babylonian religious festivals.[14]

Wink reminds his reader that the structure of "Popeye" cartoons is not unusual. It is the norm. He lists other examples that follow the same pattern. Included on this list are Green Hornet, Teenage Mutant Ninja Turtles, Superman, Superwoman, Captain Marvel, Roadrunner and many more. Variations on the theme include antiheroes like Underdog and Super Chicken whose "bumbling incompetence guarantees their victory despite themselves," as well as a recent cartoons like The Hulk or Spider Man whose heroes transform into monsters who actually do good things (through violence of course).[15]

> The format never varies. Neither party even gains insight nor learns from the encounter. Violence does not seem to teach Bluto to honor Olive Oyle's humanity and repeated pummelings do not teach Popeye to swallow the spinach before the fight.

> Only the names have changed. Marduk subdues Tiamat through violence and though he de-

feats Tiamat, chaos incessantly reasserts itself,
and is kept at bay only by repeated battles and by
the repetition of the New Year festival where the
heavenly combat is ritually reenacted.[16]

The myth of redemptive violence is not limited to cartoons. Our movies repeat this myth time and time again. These
movies begin with Clint Eastwood, Charles Bronson, Stephen
Segal or Governor Schwartzenegger experiencing an unspeakable
act of violence. This initial violent act apparently justifies the
response of the hero. Throughout much of the movie, the hero
performs even greater acts of destruction than the initial violent act
that was done by the bad guys. Finally, the ultimate battle between
the hero and the villain takes place. The hero's victory in this final
struggle restores the harmony – at least until the sequel.[17]

If this pattern were limited to entertainment, it would not
be so bad. Unfortunately, it is not. The myth of redemptive
violence governs our nation's foreign policy. For centuries, nation
after nation has embarked upon war in order to gain "security" or
restore "peace." In the early part of the 20th century, we even
fought a war to end all wars. Implicit in this grave error is the
mistaken belief that the violence of war is a sad necessity if peace
and goodness are to prevail.[18] The irony is that even "winning" a
war does little if anything to guarantee national security. In a study
of military conflict from 1500 to 2000, Paul Kennedy has
demonstrated that, at least since 1500, the nations that "won" wars
generally had their strength diminished and their security
imperiled.[19]

The myth of redemptive violence supports the dominator
system. Ultimately, this myth supports the use of violence against
those who want to end ranking. A slave who does not accept his or
her position is deemed unruly, and violence is justified against
such a person because only violence can restore the order that has
been violated. Chaos cannot be tolerated under the dominator
system. Order must always be re-established. The powers that be
often try other options to violence. They may try to "reason" with
the disorderly ones. They may even try to bribe them, but the
threat of violence always stands behind the efforts to "reason
with" or bribe those who do not know their places in the ranked
order of the dominator system.

The creation account in the first chapter of the Bible opposes the Babylonian account of creation as well as all stories that promote the myth of redemptive violence. In this story, creation is not a consequence of a violent act. It is the result of divine speech. God speaks creation into existence. God says, "Let there be light, and there was light." This is not a violent act. God speaks. Creation happens. The Biblical creation story implies that the road to peace, redemption and security is built with words. It is not paved with violence.

Western civilization finds such a statement almost incomprehensible because we depreciate words. We prefer action to words. We say, "A picture is worth 1000 words." We think that seeing is believing. It would never occur to us that hearing is believing. We get frustrated when we think we have done too much talking without "concrete results."[20] These prejudices obscure another, deeper reality about words. Words are powerful. They can destroy. They can create. They call new realities into being. Much 19th century "science fiction" is now scientific reality. It is almost as if these works of fiction called our space program into existence. By the same token, words can create psychological reality. A father who calls his son stupid, a brat or useless is far more likely to have a stupid, misbehaving or dysfunctional boy. On the other hand, a father who calls his son smart, well-behaved or industrious is far more likely to have a child that is such.

Words create social/political reality as well. Abraham Lincoln's Gettysburg address is illustrative. In the Declaration of Independence, Thomas Jefferson, a slave owner, wrote, "We hold these truths to be self-evident that all men are created equal . . ." Eighty-seven years later Abraham Lincoln said, "Four-score and seven years ago, our forefathers brought forth on this continent a new nation conceived in liberty and dedicated to the proposition that all men are created equal. . . ." Gary Wills reminds us that Abraham Lincoln's Gettysburg Address was not factually accurate, and that many of Lincoln's contemporaries said so.[21] In November of 1863, when Lincoln delivered this great speech, the United States of America had been in existence for only 74 years (three-score and fourteen). The Constitution, which created the U.S.A., was ratified in 1788. George Washington became President in 1789. Moreover, the U.S. Constitution could hardly be said to be "dedicated to the proposition that all men are created equal." The Constitution was a brilliant document, but its genius resided in its compromises. Among other things, these compromises made slavery legal, allowed the importation of African slaves until 1809, did not give women the right to vote, said nothing about the humanity of Native Americans and counted African slaves as 3/5 of a person for the purpose of congressional representation. In saying that the Declaration of Independence and not the Constitution created the United States, Lincoln gave birth to a new and different nation.

> It would have been hard to predict that Gettysburg, out of all this muddle, these missed chances, all the senseless deaths, would become a symbol of national purpose, pride and ideals. Abraham Lincoln transformed the ugly reality into something rich and strange – and he did it with 272 words. *The power of words has rarely been given a more compelling demonstration.*[22]

Lincoln's vision of America has been resisted in many ways. Indeed, a history of America's resistance to Lincoln's vision can be written in the blood of African Americans, Native Americans, workers, women and other marginalized people. Yet, Lincoln and Jefferson's words have been the standard by which we judge ourselves ever since the Gettysburg Address. Martin Luther King, Jr. articulated this vision in his famous "I Have a Dream" sermon. This is the dominant theme of the woman's movement which, incidentally and ironically, has made us realize that the statement, "all *men* are created equal," is not even in accord with its own spirit. Lincoln's words transformed America. They made America other than it would have been. They continue to oppose America's many attempts to ignore the oppressed and the marginalized, and the many times that we do so, we do so outside the spirit of America.

Such is the power of words. Words create. The power inherent in the dominator system is only the power to destroy. There is a difference between the power of words and the power that the dominator system employs. The dominator system is empowered by violence and destruction. Words empower life and new possibilities. The Biblical creation story maintains that creation owes its origin to the life-giving power of words. The Babylonian account holds that violence and death is the originating force in the cosmos. The Israelites return from their Babylonian exile with a new creation story that was diametrically opposed to the story of their former captors.

Judah's Return from Exile

Israel's return to the Promised Land was hardly spectacular. In 538 BC, the Edict of Cyrus allowed the Jewish people to return home from Babylonian exile. Many stayed. Some returned. The books of Ezra and Nehemiah are disjointed accounts of this return. It probably occurred in four stages. Following the Edict of Cyrus, a group of exiles led by Sheshhazzar returned. They started to rebuild the Temple, but they were opposed by the people living in Jerusalem and had to stop. Another group of exiles returned when Darius (521-485 BC) ruled Persia. This group was led by Zerubbabel and Jeshua. They also encountered opposition to the building of the Temple, but they were able to complete the Temple with the encouragement of the prophets Haggai and Zachariah. When Artaxerxes I (464-423 BC) ruled Persia, Nehemiah led two groups of exiles back to Jerusalem. During this period, the walls of Jerusalem were rebuilt and an attempt to reform religious and community life was initiated. Ezra may have led a fourth migration. Under the rule of Antaxerxes II (404-358 BC), the Torah (also called the Law of Moses or the first five books of the Bible) was "discovered" and read for the first time.

Israel was not an independent nation during this period. They remained under Persian rule. Indeed, Palestine remained under foreign rule for all but a century until 1948. Alexander the Great conquered the Persians in 333 BC. After he died in 323 BC, Palestine was ruled by the Ptolemies who were descendants of one of Alexander's generals. They ruled until 198 BC. The Seleucids, a family descended from another one of Alexander's generals, ruled until 166 BC when a revolt led by Judas Maccabeus established Jewish independence. This lasted until 63 BC when the Roman general Pompey conquered Jerusalem.[23]

The Jewish people remained under the dominator system throughout this time, but their subjection led them to a rather unique understanding of world history. They often viewed events and personages from the perspective of the vanquished instead of the victors. They glimpsed the dark side of the dominator system. They began to appreciate their prophets. For example, most peoples and nations thought Alexander the Great was great. The Jews understood the truth about Alexander. Alexander was a ruthless, sadistic thug. He slaughtered or subdued everything that was before him as all leaders of the dominator system had done before him and would do so after him.[24] Alexander's ruthlessness is overlooked today. We prefer to acknowledge his cultural legacy. He did, after all, "bless" the known world with the gift of Hellenism, but Hitler would have made Wagner very popular.

In any case, the Jews were in a position to understand Alexander and other tyrants differently. In the first verses of I Maccabees, we see a rare, alternative understanding of Alexander the Great.[25]

> Alexander.... fought many battles, conquered many fortresses and killed the kings of the earth. He went to the ends of the earth and plundered many nations. His ambitious heart swelled with pride when the earth fell silent before him. He gathered a powerful army. He ruled over countries, nations and princes and they paid him tribute. . .

> After ruling for twelve years, Alexander died. His officials then began to rule...They put on crowns after his death, and so did their sons and their sons after them, and they brought increasing evils into the world (I Maccabees 1:1-9).

By the time of Jesus, the dominator system ruled most of the Euro-Asian landmass. Partnership ways were barely alive in Judaism, and Judaism itself was very close to abandoning even those ways that it had had the fortune to remember. It is into this setting that Jesus calls the people of Palestine to repent.

Chapter 5:

Jesus and Partnership Ways

In the Gospel of Mark, Jesus began his public ministry proclaiming, "The time is fulfilled, the rule of God[1] is at hand, repent and believe in the gospel" (Mk. 1: 15). In the Gospel of Matthew, Jesus began saying, "Repent, for the rule of heaven is at hand" (Mt. 4: 17). These proclamations are summaries of Jesus' agenda. Jesus wanted people to repent and recognize that the rule of God was right in front of them. He wanted them to understand that they did not have to go anywhere other than where they were in order to experience God's rule. They did, however, have to repent in order to understand and experience God's rule. If they did not repent, they would not even be capable of seeing what God was doing right in front of their eyes. Some might say that the tragedy of Jesus' ministry was that the people did not repent. They crucified him instead.

The word "repent" is misinterpreted by nearly everyone. The not so religious think that repentance is a bleak experience. It is the movement from a happy fun filled life to a dark dreary existence. They get this idea from the religious ones who, when they use the word, mean that people should act in accord with some moral ideal. Many religious ones have a very interesting notion of what repentance means. When they urge some to repent, they seem to be saying, "Act more like me." This view of repentance is played out again and again in the history of religion. The Pharisees, who often opposed Jesus, clearly believed that repentance meant acting more like a Pharisee was supposed to act. Likewise, in this day and age, heterosexuals call on homosexuals to repent. By this they mean that homosexuals should act like heterosexuals (whatever that means).

This is not what Jesus meant by repentance. First and foremost, repentance means to turn around. It means to face the right direction. When Jesus told the people to repent, he was telling them to turn around. He was saying, "Do not look at the world from that perspective. Look at it this way." Repentance is at least a change of perspective. It is at least a change of worldview.

This understanding of repentance can be augmented somewhat if one also notes that the word "sin" means to miss the mark. The obvious analogy here is to that of a marksman. If we sin, we miss the target as a marksman might miss the target. Repentance is a call to turn around so that the target can at least be seen! It is not certain that a marksman will hit the target even when facing it, but it is quite certain that the target will not be hit if the marksman's back is to the target and his weapon is aimed in the wrong direction. When Jesus tells his audience to repent, he is telling them to turn around so that they can at least see the target. The problem will not even be understood if we are not facing the right direction. We cannot deal with our problem unless we repent.

Jesus still tells us to turn around so that we might understand and live life differently. We have been talking about this different understanding throughout this book. It is the paradigm shift from the dominator system to partnership ways. This shift will be addressed by viewing many aspects of Jesus' ministry. These will show that Jesus consistently lived in accord with a partnership way. He called his version of a partnership way, "the rule of God." It probably is not the only way to live in accord with a partnership way, but it is *a* way.

Jesus and Women

Since the dominator system's most fundamental form of ranking is the ranking of men above women, Jesus' relationship to women is important. To put it mildly, Jesus' relationship to women was different. In an era where women were considered no more than a man's property, Jesus had some trusted and vital relationships with women. These relationships can be seen in Scripture. Even though the Gospels were written by men under the influence of the dominator system, the Gospels cannot be told without women playing vital roles.

Mary Magdalene plays such a role. She is as much a part of Jesus' inner circle as Peter, James and John. Indeed, some have argued on the basis of recently discovered "Gospels" that the Gospel writers deliberately diminished Mary's actual role in Jesus' ministry.[2] The Gospel writers' allegiance to the dominator system with its emphasis on the subjection of women may have prevented them from adequately describing Mary's role in the circle of disciples.[3]

Mary Magdalene's important role is not even as vital to the Gospel narratives as the fact that women (Mary Magdalene was in this group) were the first witnesses to Jesus' resurrection. The importance of this fact is often lost upon us. In ancient Palestine, a "witness" who happened to be female was considered unreliable. Her testimony probably would not count in a court of law or in the Temple. The fact that women were the first witnesses to the resurrection means that for the story of Jesus to be told, the testimony of the women must be believed! Subsequent resurrection appearances only give validity to the women's initial testimony. They made the women credible witnesses. In other words, Christianity itself owes its existence to the testimony of women. Women might not be credible witnesses according ancient Palestine's version of the dominator system, but they have to be credible witnesses for the followers of Jesus. Even if the Gospel writers were male chauvinist pigs, they could not speak the Gospel without the testimony of the women.

There are many other instances in the life of Jesus that demonstrate his rather unique relationship with women, but there are none better than the incident with Mary and Martha. This story, which appears only in the Gospel of Luke, bears repeating.

> Now as they went on their way, he entered a village; and a woman named Martha received him into her house. And she had a sister called Mary, who sat at the Lord's feet and listened to his teaching. But Martha was distracted with much serving; and she went to him and said, "Lord, do you not care that my sister has left me to serve alone? Tell her then to help me." But the Lord answered her, "Martha, Martha, you are anxious and troubled about many things; one thing is needful. Mary has chosen the good portion, which shall not be taken away from her." (Lk. 10: 38-41)

It is difficult to illustrate the paradigm shift that Jesus' words create without relating a story of my own. One Saturday afternoon my two sons and I were doing yard work. The younger son was raking leaves, but the oldest was talking to me. Upon seeing us engaged in a prolonged conversation, the youngest son complained. He wanted us to get back to work. Since I had to preach on the Mary/Martha story the next day, I responded, "Gregory, Gregory, you are concerned with many things, but few things are really important. Your brother has chosen to do something very important, and I am not going to stop him." Gregory's response illumined the Mary/Martha story. He said, "Then why am I doing all this raking?"

It occurred to me that something like this was likely to have been Martha's response when she heard Jesus' words. Prior to Jesus' words to Martha, the old order had been maintained. True, Mary's presence at Jesus' feet (she was acting just like one of Jesus' disciples) was unusual. It may have been more than unusual in the culture where women were ranked below men in every social situation imaginable. Jesus' reply to Martha, however, demonstrates that Jesus is living outside this order. It leaves Martha wondering why she is doing all the work while everyone else just sits around listening to Jesus.

Martha's consciousness is altered. She has two choices inside this new paradigm. First, she can stop performing her social role. She too can stop working and sit down and listen to what Jesus is saying. This action would create a variety of problems for those gathered. The male disciples, for example, would start wondering if they were going to be fed! Knowing these disciples, it would probably take them some time before they realized that they might actually have to do something. If they were still in bondage to the dominator system, they would probably suggest leaving to find a household where women knew their place. If they were somewhat liberated from the dominator system, these guys might decide to do the "women's work" necessary to at least put a meal on the table. Martha's second choice could be to continue doing what she was doing. Now, however, she continues because she chooses to do so. Social custom and patriarchy do not compel her. She works as a free person who can stop at any time.

The Mary/Martha episode attacks the very foundation of the dominator system. As we have seen, ranking is the most fundamental characteristic of this system, and the ranking of men above women is the most basic sort of ranking.[4] Jesus' reply to Martha's request creates a new order of things. Jesus upholds

Mary's discipleship, and Jesus liberates Martha from her slavery to the dominator system. He does so using a creative word that reminds us of the sort of word that God used in creation. This word is not a violent act. It is a word that creates something new. In this case, Jesus' reply re-establishes the partnership way.

Jesus' Parables

Jesus taught using parables. His parabolic style is itself interesting because parables are always ambiguous. They have no clear-cut meaning, and they can be interpreted in a variety of ways. *If Jesus was concerned about communicating one unambiguous and crystal clear message, he would not have taught in parables.*

Parables are confusing for a variety of reasons. Sometimes they are confusing because the facts a parable narrates are inaccurate. An example of such a parable is the parable of the mustard seed (Mk. 4: 30-32). Here Jesus compares the rule of God to a mustard seed, which, Jesus says, "is the smallest seed in the world," and grows to become the "biggest of all plants." Well, the fact is that the mustard seed is not the smallest seed in the world, and no amount of exegesis can make it the smallest seed in the world. Moreover, the mustard seed does not become the biggest of all plants. Perhaps Jesus' audience did not know smaller seeds than the mustard seed, but they had to know that the mustard plant was not the biggest of all plants. Their lives were filled with examples of many plants bigger than the mustard plant.

One of the many ways to interpret this parable is to imagine the reaction of the people who knew very well that the mustard plant was not the largest plant in the world. On the one hand, a listener might say that the parable is crazy and wonder what is wrong with the guy who tells them this parable. At least he should get his facts about plant sizes straight. On the other hand, the audience might understand the parable differently. Knowing that the mustard plant is by far one of the smaller plants, but hearing that the rule of God is like a mustard seed that grows into the largest of all plants, the audience might conclude that Jesus is talking about the rule of God and not the mustard plant. They might think that like this unusual mustard seed, the rule of God is a fantastic surprise. It looks ordinary. It looks small. Since the rule of God has such an ordinary in appearance, everyone thinks it is predictable; however, they are in for a big surprise. The rule of God is far beyond their wildest expectations. More can be said about this short parable, but enough has been said to illustrate that parables strike the imagination. They free the mind. They allow people to envision new things, and in the case of the parable of the mustard seed, these new things are envisioned precisely because Jesus has narrated facts that are known by his audience to be inaccurate.

Sometimes parables are odd because they discuss situations where the reasoning process of the people involved leaves much to be desired. The parable of the tenants in the vineyard is a good example.

> A man planted a vineyard, and set a hedge around it, and dug a pit for the wine press, and built a tower, and let it out to tenants, and went to another country. When the time came, he sent a servant to the tenants, to get from them some of the fruit of the vineyard. And they took him and beat him, and sent him away empty-handed. Again he sent to them another servant, and they wounded him in the head, and treated him shamefully. And he sent another, and him they killed; and so with many others, some they beat and some they killed. He had still one other, a beloved son; finally he sent him to them, saying, "They will respect my son." But those tenants said to one another, "This is the heir; come, let us kill him, and the inheritance will be ours." And they took him and killed him, and cast him out of the vineyard. (Mk. 12: 1-8)

A few things must be kept in mind when discussing this or any other parable. First, the Gospel writers were not journalists who followed Jesus around recording his words and actions. They were people who wrote about Jesus 30 or 40 years after his death. Each Gospel writer has a reason for writing. Each arranged the stories and teachings of Jesus in a way that suited his purpose. Second, one must also recognize the fact – and it is a fact – that quotation marks were not invented when the Gospel writers wrote. They were probably not invented until the printing press. This means that all quotation marks were placed in position nearly 1500 years after the original text was written. Quotations marks are, therefore, reasonably accurate at the beginning of the quotation because they follow words like said or asked. They are not as accurate at the end of one of Jesus' speeches, statements or parables. In other words, it is much easier to determine where Jesus starts to speak than it is to determine where Jesus stops speaking. It is always an interpretation of someone other than the author as to where Jesus' words end.

In so far as the parable under consideration is concerned, it is my opinion that the parable ends in verse 8 (the place where the above quotation ends). There are two reasons for this. First, the Gospel of Thomas – an account of Jesus' life that is not in Scripture but written before the Gospels of Matthew Mark and Luke – indicates that the parable ends here. Second, the interpretation of the parable that is present in Mark tends to make the story into an allegory instead of a parable. What appears to be Mark's interpretation of Jesus' parable is as follows:

> What will the owner of the vineyard do? He will come and destroy the tenants and give the vineyard to others. Have you not read this in Scripture? "The very stone which the builders rejected has become the corner; this was the Lord's doing, and it is amazing in our eyes" (Mk. 12: 9-11).

As just stated, Mark's interpretation makes Jesus' parable into an allegory. Allegories are stories in which every important element in the story corresponds to something "in real life." The meanings allegories seek to communicate are quite inescapable once it is known what corresponds to what. The parable in question is simple and clear-cut if it is interpreted as an allegory. The owner of the vineyard is God. The vineyard is the land of Israel. The tenants are the Jews or Jewish leaders. The slaves sent by the owner are the prophets. The son who is sent by the owner and killed by the tenants is Jesus. The new owners to whom the owner will give the vineyard are the Christians.

Interpreted in this way, the parable merely takes on the ideology of the Christians of the late first century. They believed, as many still do, that God gave Israel a trust. They violated their trust even though God repeatedly sent prophets. Finally God had enough. He sent his son Jesus, and they killed Jesus. As a consequence, the trust once given to Israel was transferred to the Church which understands itself as the new Israel. Interpreting this parable as an allegory was an agenda of the early Church. It is often argued that the parallels to this parable in Matthew and Luke (Mt. 21: 33-46 and Lk. 20: 9-19) make the connections between the characters in the parable and characters in reality far more explicit.[5]

It is always in the interest of the dominator system to interpret a parable as if it were an allegory. The reason for this is simple. Allegorical interpretations leave nothing to the imagination. Once the connections have been made between the characters in the story and those outside the story, nothing more can be said. Indeed, insofar as the relationship between Christianity and Judaism is concerned, nothing more was ever said about the relationship between the two religions almost until the present moment. The Church has yet to overcome the anti-Semitism present in our allegorical interpretation of this parable. Such an interpretation continues to assist the dominator system's effort to draw the line that separates the good from the bad, the saints from the sinners and the Christians from the Jews. It will always be easier for Christians to treat the Jews in an inhuman manner as long as such allegorical interpretations exist.

Interpreting this story as a parable, however, yields different results. For example, our allegorical interpretation has equated the owner of the vineyard with God. If the owner is just a guy who planted a vineyard, however, we are far more likely to see the absolute insanity of his actions. He sends a slave to collect the rent. The slave gets beaten and sent back. So, like the intellectual giant he is, the owner sends another slave and gets similar results. The owner then appears to reason that if sending slaves does not work, the wise thing to do is to send more slaves! He does so, and "surprisingly" some slaves are beaten and others are killed. A note of caution is in order here. Do not think that it is unusual to keep on doing that which has been proven not to work. This appears to be the policy of many organizations. Our educational systems are not teaching many children the basic skills like reading, writing and arithmetic. So, our natural response is to spend more money doing more of what has been proven not to work. This probably happens in business, sports and families as well. When faced with failure, we often work harder doing the very things that brought on the failure in the first place. We are like the owner of the vineyard who kept sending slaves even though that tactic had failed on numerous occasions. If we put the matter in this context, the owner still looks pretty stupid, but he does not look that unusual.

To the owner's credit, after failure upon failure and disaster after disaster, he does change his policy. His brilliant mind leads him to the conclusion that instead of sending his slaves he will send his beloved son. What could possibly happen? Once again, if we interpret the parable as an allegory that reinforces Christian anti-Semitism, we are prevented from seeing just how insane the owner's new plan is because we assume we are dealing with an all-knowing God. Freed from our bondage to allegorical interpretations, however, we now find nothing in the history of the owner's relationship with his tenants that would lead him to believe that his son would be treated well. As a matter of fact, everything indicated that he was putting his son in danger. Nonetheless, in his infinite wisdom, the owner sent his son. Now the scene shifts to the tenants.

The reasoning of the tenants also leaves much to be desired. Even though there is no reason to think so, these people believe that they will actually inherit the vineyard if they kill the landlord's son. One wonders how anyone could possibly arrive at such a conclusion. Once again, however, there are parallels in contemporary culture. Several years ago a group of people in San Diego California convinced themselves that if they killed themselves (they called it "shed their containers"), they would somehow achieve a higher state of consciousness. This higher consciousness would unite them with aliens who were somehow associated with a large comet that was approaching the earth. I probably have not accurately summarized their theology, but the fact of the matter is these people convinced themselves that mass suicide was the rational thing to do at that precise moment. Moreover, people who were part of this group but not present in San Diego still lament the fact that they missed the opportunity to "shed their containers."

The tenants in our parable remind us that people are capable of believing just about anything when they cut themselves off from the rest of the world. This often happens in small groups that isolate themselves, but it is true of larger groups as well. It happens between religions where one group believes another worthy of death because they have slightly different doctrines. It happens in entire nations that convince themselves that building more and more armaments is the path to peace. In many cases, our reasoning processes mimic that of the tenants. As a whole, human beings are capable of believing just about anything. There is hardly an absurdity that if repeated often enough will not be believed or acted upon by one person or another.

A final question to consider is, "Why does everyone in the parable seem to be so stupid?" Not only do the tenants and the landlord exhibit serious mental defects, but all the slaves – with the possible exception of the first two slaves sent to collect the rent – do not appear to have "all their oars in the water." The son is clearly related to his father. Their similarity in intellectual capacities is seen when the son agrees to go and collect the rent.

There are many possible answers to this question, but an answer that is faithful to the parable is required. This means that the attempt must be made to answer this question using the material the parable presents. One cannot make up stories about all the difficulties the landlord faced in his childhood. One should not invent a system of law whereby the tenants would actually inherit the vineyard. (They may have been able to steal the vineyard. They could not inherit it.) A faithful interpretation of the parable requires that we focus on the parable itself.

If we focus on the parable, we find that the only constant in this story is the vineyard. In this parable, the vineyard is not Israel. It is just a vineyard. What ever else a vineyard is, it is an agricultural enterprise, and everyone associated with this enterprise cannot think straight. The inability of those associated with the vineyard to think straight is related to the construction of the vineyard itself. The vineyard has a fence around it. The fence is designed to protect the crop from harm. As those who put fences around gardens know, the protection a fence accords is protection from human beings and animals. Building a vineyard puts us at war with anything in nature that will damage the crop.[6] This implies that we will view both people and nature as potential enemies. Rather than being a part of nature or in community with other human beings, the vineyard makes us view those outside as alien.

The building of the watchtower admits such fears. The watchtower enables the inhabitants of the vineyard to see enemies approaching and to prepare a defense. In this case, the watchtower probably allowed the tenants to see the son coming and work on their vicious scheme with its crazy rationale.

Building a vineyard was a normal thing to do. It is a product of the agricultural revolution. In this parable we see the dark side of normal. The vineyard creates a "we versus they" mentality. Those on the "outside" – be they man or beast – are understood as a threat to the way of life of those on the inside. The fence around the perimeter of the vineyard separates the "good guys" from the "bad guys." Every effort is made to defend the inside from the pollution that the outside can bring.

There are many parallels between this parable and what happens in the world. Fences are built between religions like Islam and Christianity, Judaism and Christianity, Islam and Judaism and Hinduism and Islam. Within Christianity, fences are built between denominations. Everyone engaged in such practices develops inaccurate images of the "outsiders," and they act on them in ways that are not unlike the ways of the owner and tenants in the vineyard. Just how much this tendency to draw the line separating "the good" from "the bad" is a by-product of the agricultural revolution's need to keep food "under lock and key" is debatable. What is not debatable is the fact that the drawing of such lines or the building of such fences is the most basic function of the dominator system. Ranking begins with the line that separates the good from the bad. It proceeds to draw lines that determine the better from the merely acceptable and the best from the better. If the parable is correct, the drawing of such lines or the building of such fences is also behind the strange ways we human beings think.

There are a number of faithful ways that this parable or any parable can be interpreted. Indeed, this might be the first time that this particular parable has ever been interpreted in this way. Parables are like poems or paintings or other works of art. There is always more that can be said about great poems and paintings.[7] As a matter of fact, what makes a work of art great is the fact that there is always more that can be told about the poem or work of art. This is how it is with Jesus' parables. There is always more that can be said about one of his parables. This is because, like a

93

great work of art, Jesus' parables inspire the imagination. They free the human mind. A free mind is a mind capable of envisioning alternatives to the established order of things.

Jesus parabolic speech mimics God's words in creation. As the Word of God brought creation into being, Jesus' words bring forth new possibilities. They strike the imagination. They begin creative processes.

It is not in the interest of the dominator model to speak in parabolic form. The dominator system wants to leave nothing to the imagination. It desires to have a monopoly on language and thought as well as on actions.[9] It fears the alternatives to the dominant order that can be dreamed by an inspired imagination because once an alternative is stated it becomes easier to bring it into being. This is why adherents of the dominator system from Plato to Stalin have always feared poetry and persecuted artists. This is also why Jesus was opposed by the powers that be. It is also why the powers that be killed him. His words set the imagination free. His words allowed people to envision alternatives. This is the greatest threat to those who think that there is only one way to live and think.

Jesus and Morality

This may come as a shock to religious people and non-religious people alike, but Jesus was not a moral person. Jesus was not immoral either. The morally good and upright people accused him of immorality, but Jesus was not immoral. Jesus was ethical.[10] Obviously, distinguishing between moral and ethical is confusing. The English language suggests no difference exists between the moral and ethical, however, such a distinction needs to be made if we are to adequately describe Jesus. The following is an effort to do so despite the limitations of our language.

We have already exposed the dark side of morality. We have argued that morality began when food was commoditized. The moment food became something that was bought and sold criteria were developed that determined who would receive food and who would not. Morality emerges when these criteria are rationalized, and this rationalization is usually done by religious and intellectual leaders.

Two characteristics of morality emerge as a consequence. First, morality is intimately related to death because it determines who gets fed and who starves. Moreover, when morality draws the line between those worthy of food and those who are not, it calls those worthy of food "good" and the unworthy "bad." This designation gives the "good" and well fed the right to kill or neglect the "bad" and hungry. Second, what is "good" in one culture may be "evil" in another because the criteria whereby people are judged worthy to receive food differ from culture to culture. The world has never had a universal morality, however, people as diverse as Plato, President Bush and Osama bin Laden have thought that their individual moralities are universal and should be imposed on the rest of the world. While the content of these moral beliefs are not the same, differing moralities perform the same, universal function. They always tell their adherents who they should protect and who they can leave for dead. Forget the fact that George Bush's morality states that it is a righteous act to kill Osama bin Laden, and that Osama's morality states that it is righteous to kill George Bush. Both moralities draw the line between the good guys and the bad guys. They just believe that different people are good and different people are bad. It has been this way since food became a commodity.

Jesus was not moral because he did not engage in the most fundamental aspect of morality. He did not draw the line that separated the good from the bad or the clean from the unclean. His culture clearly drew this line. His culture drew the line between the sick and the healthy. It taught that the sick were unclean and that illness was evidence of the sick person's sin. It taught that the sick could not be touched. Nevertheless, Jesus often healed the sick with a touch. Jesus' culture also despised tax collectors. They were thought to be traitors and extortionists. Jesus ate with tax collectors. He made one or two his disciples. Jesus' culture also thought prostitutes were sinners and unclean, but it is said that Mary Magdalene was a prostitute. She was also one of the people closest to Jesus.

Karl Marx demonstrated to the modern world (as the prophet Amos showed Israel) that those who fall on the wrong side of morality's line are not necessarily there because they are evil. More often than not, they are there because of social oppression. This has led some under the influence of Marx to identify with the poor and oppressed. Like Jesus, these people associate with the poor and marginalized and try to help them with their plight. Their distinction from Jesus can be noted in their tendency to call the poor and oppressed "good" and the rich and powerful "bad." In other words, they maintain the moral divide. The people once on the "good" side of the line now are on the "bad" side of the line, but the line itself continues to exist. Unlike Jesus, these social activists remain moral because they maintain the moral divide. The line between the good and the bad is the basic, most fundamental tenant of morality.

Jesus is not moral because he never drew the line separating the good from the bad. He ate with sinners. He cured the sick. Conversely, he also associated with the rich, powerful and religious leaders. He engaged them in conversation. He ate at their tables. He answered their questions. He forgave his executioners. Morality's line does not exist for Jesus. He does not draw that line. While people may cut themselves off from Jesus, he does not retaliate. He is not moral. If, as the Church says, Jesus "is without sin," this is the sense in which he is without sin. He does not draw morality's line. He never succumbed to the power of the fruit of the Tree of the Knowledge of Good and Evil.

This being said, there is a definite and discernable preference for the poor, the marginalized, the sick and even the immoral in Jesus' ministry. The rich, powerful and religious think Jesus is a threat. The poor, oppressed and immoral find no threat in Jesus. This is not because Jesus hates the rich and loves the poor. It is because Jesus is ethical and not moral. An ethical person refuses to draw lines separating the good from the bad. This refusal leads one to associate with those who morality's line has left for dead. This threatens people who benefit from morality's sanctions. They fear the loss of morality's sanction. They cannot understand how they will live if they lose this sanction. Thus, they oppose Jesus. The one dimensional dominator system leaves them no alternative. Either they are on the right side of the line or they will be left for dead. Jesus, however, presents an alternative. It is an ethical alternative in which no lines are drawn.

Jesus expresses his opposition to morality in several ways. One of the most important is the way he deals with direct moral questions. To be succinct, Jesus never directly answers a moral question. One of the most pervasive moral questions facing the

Jews in first century Palestine was the question of paying taxes. The Herodian party said that taxes to Rome should be paid. The Pharisees thought otherwise. The argument was constant, and the Pharisees and Herodians often disputed bitterly about this and other moral concerns. Jesus had a way of uniting enemies, and apparently he united the Herodians and the Pharisees. Unfortunately, he united these powerful groups against himself. Matthew 25: 15-22 tells of an event in which these two parties tried to trap Jesus. Both parties got together and asked Jesus if it was lawful to pay taxes to the Roman Emperor. They wanted a simple yes or no. They got something quite different. Jesus asked them to show him a coin. He asked whose face was on the coin. He was told that it was the Emperor's face. Jesus told them to "render unto Caesar the things that are Caesar's and to God the things that are God's." In short, Jesus did not answer the question!

His response did two things, however. First, it recognized that there is a difference between God and our rulers. Our rulers wish we would forget this distinction. Second, Jesus' response leaves it to our own mind to figure out the relationship between God and government. Ironically, this was the exact problem that Jesus' questioners wanted him to answer when they asked if it was lawful to pay taxes.

Jesus refused to answer this question because he was not a moral person. Answering the question would have drawn the line separating the good from the bad. If Jesus had said you should pay taxes, those who refused to pay would have been judged immoral. If Jesus had said that taxes should not be paid, those who paid would be judged immoral. In not answering the question, Jesus did not deem anyone moral or immoral, and he left it up to the person and the person's community to determine when and if taxes should be paid. Presumably, Jesus left open the possibility that taxes should be paid sometimes and not paid at other times. The issue depends on the relationship between God and government at a given time and place.

At another time and place, Jesus was approached by a teacher of the Torah who asked what he must do to receive eternal life. Jesus did not answer him. Instead he asked the question, "What do Scriptures say? How do *you* interpret them?" (Lk. 10: 26). The teacher of the Law said, "Love the Lord your God with all your heart, with all your soul, with all your strength and with all your mind and love your neighbor as yourself" (Lk. 10: 27). Jesus told him that he was right. Apparently, the teacher of the Torah thought he had no problems loving God with all his heart, soul, strength and mind, but he was not so sure about the neighbor part. Luke tells us that "in an effort to justify himself" he asked Jesus, "Who is my neighbor." The teacher of the Torah probably thought that if he could just get Jesus to define neighbor, then loving one's neighbor would be a little easier. If he could get Jesus to say that these people are neighbors and those people are not, the teacher could go about the business of loving those designated as neighbor and forgetting about those who were not so designated. In short, he wanted Jesus to draw the line that marks off this man's neighbors from his non-neighbors. Then he would be responsible only for those designated neighbors. He could treat the others as if they did not exist.

Jesus does not give the teacher of the Torah what he wanted. He did not define neighbor and thereby draw the line that marks off this man's neighbors from his non-neighbors. Instead, Jesus told the following story.

> A man was going down from Jerusalem to Jericho, and he fell among robbers, who stripped him and beat him, and departed, leaving him half dead. Now by chance a priest was going down that road; and when he saw him, he passed by on the other side. So likewise, a Levite, when he came to the place and saw him, passed by on the other side. But a Samaritan, as he journeyed, came to where he was; and when he saw him, he had compassion, and went to him and bound up his wounds, pouring on oil and wine; then he set him on his own beast and brought him to an inn, and took care of him. And the next day he took out two denarii and gave them to the innkeeper, saying, "Take care of him; and whatever more you spend, I will repay you when I come back." Which of these three, do you think, proved neighbor to the man who fell among the robbers? He said, "The one who showed mercy on him. And Jesus said to him, "Go and do likewise." (Lk. 10: 30-37).

This story is so familiar that many people cannot feel the impact of the story on those who first heard it. For example, we routinely use the phrase "Good Samaritan." We name hospitals Good Samaritan Hospital. We think the words "good" and "Samaritan" go together. For the Jew living in first century Palestine, however, this was not the case. Samaritans were the enemy. They were a religious threat. The word good never would be used as an adjective modifying Samaritan in any sentence uttered by a first century Palestinian Jew. It would be like us telling a story about a good terrorist or a friendly hit man.

When the teacher of the Torah asked Jesus to define neighbor, he was inviting Jesus to serve the dominator system by drawing a line that separated neighbor from non-neighbor. Perhaps the teacher expected people like the Priest and Levite – the orthodox ones – to be on the neighbor side of the line. It never would have occurred to him that a Samaritan could ever be considered his neighbor. His answer that the one who acted as neighbor was the one who showed mercy recognizes that the unthinkable had happened. A Samaritan had been revealed to be a neighbor. Moreover, the Samaritan was the neighbor because he had shown mercy.

In the context of the struggle between the dominator system and partnership ways, this is a significant admission. A merciful act is an act that disregards any distinction a person or culture might make between the worthy ones and the unworthy ones. Indeed, mercy is not something someone deserves. If you deserve to be treated in a particular way and are treated that way, the act is not merciful. Thus, if the neighbor is the one who shows mercy, a neighbor is someone who does not live according to the lines drawn by the dominator system. One who shows mercy disregards such demarcations. One who shows mercy refuses to allow ranking to dictate his or her behavior toward others. The Samaritan was such a man. Samaritans, after all, felt the same way about the Jews as the Jews felt about them. If a Samaritan were to draw a line separating neighbors from non-neighbors, Jews would clearly be on the non-neighbor side of this moral divide. This divide had no impact on the Good Samaritan. He showed mercy. The Good Samaritan found no value in a moral system that would leave someone for dead.

In the final analysis, the story of the Good Samaritan is correctly interpreted by the teacher of the Torah and not by Jesus. It is the teacher who says that the neighbor is the one who shows mercy. This, however, is not a definition of the word neighbor. It is an analysis of the activity of being a neighbor. A neighbor is one who is merciful. That is to say that a neighbor is one who shows mercy to those who the moral, political and religious institutions of the dominator system have left for dead.

On many occasions, it has been stated that moralities differ from culture to culture because the criteria that determines one's worthiness for food differs from culture to culture. Ethical activity is different. It always involves showing mercy to those who the moral, political and religious institutions of the dominator system have left for dead. Unlike the different moralities of the dominator system, the ethics of partnership ways – the ethics Jesus promoted – always involve mercy. Accordingly, ethical behavior, in contrast to moral behavior, is absolute.[11] It always involves acting mercifully to those who the dominator system leaves for dead. It always involves disregarding the line that separates the good from the bad, the rich from the poor, the powerful from the oppressed, the clean from the unclean and the worthy from the unworthy.

Jesus' parable of the Laborers in the Vineyard dramatically illustrates how an act of mercy undermines the way we normally function under the dominator system. This parable begins with the words, "The rule of God is like this." The parable proceeds to establish the sharp contrast between this rule of God and life under the dominator system.

> The rule of God is like a householder who went out early in the morning to hire laborers for his vineyard. After agreeing with the laborers for a denarius a day, he sent them into his vineyard. And going out about the third hour he saw others standing idle in the market place; and to them he said, "You go into the vineyard too, and whatever is right I will give you." So they went. Going out again about the sixth hour and the ninth hour, he did the same. And about the eleventh hour he went out and found others standing; and he said to them, "Why do you stand here idle all day?" they

said to him, "Because no one has hired us." He said to them, "You go into the vineyard too." And when evening came, the owner of the vineyard said to his steward, "Call the laborers and pay them their wages, beginning with the last, up to the first." And when those hired about the eleventh hour came, each of them received a denarius. Now when the first came, they thought they would receive more; but each of them also received a denarius. And on receiving it they grumbled at the householder, saying, "these last worked only one hour, and you have made them equal to us who have borne the burden of the day and the scorching heat." But he replied to one of them, "Friend, I am doing you no wrong; did you not agree with me for a denarius? Take what belongs to you, and go; I choose to give to this last as I give to you. Am I not allowed to do what I choose with what belongs to me? Or do you begrudge my generosity?" (Mt. 20: 1-14)

Nearly everyone thinks that there is something quite wrong with the owner's behavior in this parable. True, he did meet his contractual obligations. He paid those who had worked the entire day the agreed upon amount. Yet, nearly everyone thinks that some kind of injustice has been done in this parable.

The story is made even more disagreeable because the owner could have avoided the conflict with the laborers who had worked all day by simply paying them first. He could have paid them and sent them home. Then he could have given those who did not work the entire day whatever he pleased. The owner does not even take this route. As a matter of fact, he deliberately paid those who had worked fewer hours before he paid those who had worked all day. He appears to have wanted those who had worked the longest to *see* that he was paying the latecomers the same amount they would receive.

The reason almost everyone thinks that there is something wrong here is that we and the laborers who had worked all day prefer the morality of the dominator system to the mercy of God. It is our preference for ranking that tells us that something is amiss in this story. Ranking tells us that those who work longer are "better" or more deserving than those who do not work as long. Our morality demands that the ones who work longer deserve higher status and more money. Ranking creates the illusion that we deserve whatever we have because we have fulfilled obligations based upon one moral code or another. (In this case the code is based upon the time one has worked). The owner does not operate according to this code. Instead of giving what was "earned," he gives what was needed. (It is generally thought that one denarius was the amount of money a Palestinian family needed to make it through the day). In giving what was needed rather than what was deserved, the owner was acting in accord with "the rule of God." He showed mercy, and thereby, rejected the merciless morality of the dominator system.

This parable reveals both our resistance to mercy and to the rule of God. Those who resist, resist because they do not think they need mercy. Morality creates this illusion by suggesting that a person's moral worth is entirely within his or her control. External conditions are not considered. The line establishing one's worthiness has been drawn, and those who fall on the "worthy" side of the line will resent the "unworthy" when they receive grace or mercy. This is how the dominator system cultivates its allies. Mercy and grace are rarely thought desirable by people who consider themselves morally worthy. Such people think that they owe their success to hard work. They do not believe that they have been recipients of mercy and grace. They believe they deserve everything they have received. Accordingly, they do not like mercy and grace because it undermines the way they live.

This fact is true in all spheres of life that are under the dominator system. Religious people who think that they have made themselves worthy by virtue of their prayers, mature spiritual life or generosity have a great deal of difficulty with a merciful God. Like those in the parable who have born the heat of the day, they cannot help but wonder why they have done all they have done if God grants mercy to those less worthy than they. They have the same attitude as those who worked all day in the parable. They do not care if people live or die. They only care that the rules are followed. They think that justice demands that they receive more than those who accomplished less.

Actually justice does demand that they receive more, but the sort of justice that demands this is always associated with the dominator system. This system demands that a line be drawn separating the worthy from the unworthy. This system holds out the possibility that the unworthy can become worthy by meeting the criteria the culture establishes for one's worthiness, however, this system has no mercy for those failing to meet its moral criteria. *The parable of the Laborers in the Vineyard understands justice differently. Here justice involves giving what is needed.* This sort of justice disregards the moral divide drawn by dominator cultures. This sort of justice treats those deemed unworthy with grace and mercy. Those who benefit from the dominator system (or hope that one day they might benefit) oppose grace and mercy. Political and religious leaders have always been included in this group. These are the ones who, despite their many differences, united to execute Jesus. They had to do so because Jesus proclaimed the rule of God. He spoke of a partnership way. This has always been the ultimate threat to the dominator system and to those benefiting from this system.

Jesus and Religion

It was not Jesus' goal to create a new religion called Christianity. Jesus was a Jew. Jesus remained a Jew. He did not reject Judaism. He never became a Christian. He did, however, oppose certain religious practices present within Judaism and other religions when they serve the dominator system.

The story called "the Cleansing of the Temple" illustrates Jesus' opposition to religion in the service of the dominator system. This story is told in all four Gospels (Mt. 21: 12-16; Mk. 11: 15-18; Lk. 19: 45-48; Jn. 2: 13-16). Its structure is as follows. Jesus enters the Temple. He gets angry. He upsets the tables of the moneychangers. He drives out everyone who is selling things. He may have liberated a few doves and a couple of sheep. Finally, Jesus interpreted his actions with words from the prophets Isaiah and Jeremiah when he said, "Is it not written, (God's) house shall be a house of prayer for all nations. But you have made it a den of thieves." This story vividly illustrates Jesus' opposition to religion in the service of the dominator system. Such religion was being practiced by Jesus' contemporaries and is currently practiced by most Western religions today.

Jesus' opposition to religion that serves the dominator system can be illustrated in some of the "business" practices surrounding the Temple's rituals. In the Gospel of Luke, for example, Mary and Joseph took their baby Jesus to the Temple in Jerusalem to perform the rite of purification (Lk. 2: 22-24). This rite required that a pair of doves be offered as a sacrifice. Mary and Joseph probably did not raise these doves from chicks and carry them from Nazareth to Jerusalem. More likely they purchased the doves in the Temple courtyard. In the Temple courtyard there were people who would sell animals like sheep and doves for the purpose of sacrifice. They made sure that the animals met the specifications of the Torah and were acceptable sacrifices. In other words, the people who sold animals for sacrifice were performing a much needed service. People did not have to raise the sacrificial animals themselves. They did not have to transport them to the Temple, and they could be sure of the animal's quality.

Additionally, the Torah (also called the Law of Moses or the first five books of the Bible) specified that only a certain kind of money could be used to purchase the animals for sacrifice. Hence, the moneychangers also provided a much needed service. For a small fee, they would take coins from one place and exchange them for coins that were acceptable Temple currency. When Jesus got angry and drove the moneychangers and those selling animals out of the Temple, he was temporarily stopping the Temple's sacrificial worship practices. This was a symbolic act. The moneychangers and others quickly resumed their practices. Nonetheless, Jesus' opposition to religion based on sacrifice was clearly expressed in this action.

In opposing sacrificial worship practices, Jesus was acting squarely within his Jewish tradition. Examples of this fact abound. The prophet Amos wrote:

> "The Lord says, 'I despise your feasts, and I take no delight in your solemn assemblies. Even though you offer me your burnt offerings and cereal offerings, I will not accept them, and the peace offerings of your fatted beasts I will not look upon. Take away from me the noise of your songs; to the melody of your harps I will not listen. But let justice roll down like waters, and

righteousness like an ever-flowing stream."
(Amos 5:21-24).

Jeremiah asks, "Will you steal, murder, commit adultery, swear falsely, burn incense to Ba'al and go after other gods that you have not known and then come and stand before me in this house, which is called by my name, and say, 'We are delivered!' – only to go on doing all these abominations?" (Jr. 7: 8 - 10). It is interesting to note that Jeremiah then goes on to say that the Temple has become a den of robbers. (Jr. 7: 11).

Jesus and the prophets opposed sacrificial religion because it gave people a license to do whatever they pleased. Once a sacrifice was made, obligations to God were fulfilled. A person could rely on God's favor. A person did not have to worry about offending God, so the person could do whatever he or she pleased. Sacrificial religion functioned to protect people from God as bribes might be employed to protect criminals from the police, or a hideout might protect thieves from detection. This is why Jeremiah and Jesus said that their religious leaders had turned the Temple from a house of prayer into a den of thieves.

Sacrificial worship provides religious justification for morality by giving the rules of morality the appearance of divine sanction. Accordingly, sacrificial worship assists the dominator system. It grants divine sanction to the arbitrary standards by which a given culture ranks, and it helps the economic and political powers maintain their position of dominance. Historically, Christianity has functioned in this way. It too asks that Christians perform certain sacrifices to placate the deity. The medieval church, for example, maintained God demanded complete obedience. Since no one ever gave God complete obedience, everyone fell short. The Church, however, had a deposit of merits that it could use to make up the difference between the individual's actual obedience and the complete obedience that God demanded. In order to obtain these needed merits, the Church instituted a system whereby these merits could be obtained if certain actions or sacrifices were performed. This system served the dominator system because it clearly taught that the performance of certain practices merited divine favor. This enabled the line to be established between those who merited divine favor and those who did not.

Protestants would like to think that the Reformation abolished these sacrificial practices. Following Martin Luther, Protestants have held that people are justified by faith and not by certain practices that merit divine favor. More often than not, however, justification by faith – the central tenant of the Reformation – is thought to mean that we merit divine favor if we have faith. In such instance, a person's faith is merely a substitute for other sacrifices the medieval Church demanded. In other words, the *quid pro quo* structure of sacrificial worship is maintained. The only difference is that the task that a person has to perform in order to merit divine favor is different. The line that separates the good from the bad is still intact. Christianity still serves the dominator system.

Christianity will serve the dominator system as long it continues to draw lines that separate the good from the bad, the worthy from the unworthy and the saved from the damned. The dominator system does not care what criteria are used to draw this line. It does not matter if the line is drawn because of some "virtuous" action on our part. It does not matter if the line is drawn by virtue of birthright. It does not matter to the dominator system if the line is drawn on the basis of correct belief or correct doctrine. It does not matter if the line is drawn when we sacrifice a turtledove. It does not matter if God draws the line by arbitrarily choosing some and not others. The issue is the existence of the line separating the worthy from the unworthy. Wherever this line exists, religion serves the dominator system. Wherever this line exists, religion can become the source of war and violence or its justification. If this line did not exist, September 11, 2001 would have just been another day.

In the cleansing of the Temple, Jesus attacked this moral divide. Indeed, his entire ministry was an assault on this line. He ate with the clean and the unclean. He partied with sinners. He invited association with the religious people of his day. He even refused to be called "good" (Mk. 10: 18). *This was not a rejection of his Jewish traditions. Jesus was squarely in the midst of a Jewish tradition that believed that Judaism was to be a blessing to all nations rather than an island of the chosen in the midst of the God forsaken. Jesus was rejecting Judaism's subservience to the dominator system when he refused to make a moral divide.* The prophets also rejected such expressions of Judaism. They too opposed establishing a line separating the worthy from the unworthy. They too rejected the dominator system's control of Judaism.

Jesus and Power

In an address called "Two Kinds of Power," Bernard Loomer distinguishes between unilateral power and communal power. The dominator system employs unilateral power. It is the "capacity to influence, guide, adjust, manipulate, shape, control or transform the human or natural environment in order to advance one's own purposes."[12] Loomer calls unilateral power one dimensional because it involves moving and influencing others without being subject to the influence of others. Accordingly, inequality and ranking are two inherent features of this sort of power; hence, concerns about status, station and rank have always been central to those who exercise unilateral power. Unilateral power's focus on ranking indicates its service to the dominator system.

Those possessing unilateral power rarely relinquish it voluntarily. In a system where a person's dignity, status and rank depend on one's position, relinquishing unilateral power is the same as relinquishing rank and status. As a consequence, concessions are seldom voluntary. They come only when rivals possess enough unilateral power to force such concessions.[13] Few social changes occur as a consequence of someone voluntarily relinquishing unilateral power. Agents of social change like labor unions and civil rights groups first develop their own power base and then use this newly created power to gain concessions. Saul Alinsky was absolutely correct when he observed that (under the dominator system) people with power will only listen if the opposition has enough political clout to make them listen. There is an important corollary to this statement. Those possessing unilateral power will remain indifferent to those who can safely be ignored.[14] Unilateral power can safely ignore the poor, who are silenced by the weight of their poverty, as well as generations yet to be born. These voiceless ones are always ignored even in the most "liberal" democracies.

Unilateral power kills. Its ability to kill is the source of its power. Unilateral power originates in an unmoved center and is directed against an external world. Those using unilateral power try to move or manipulate the external world without being moved themselves.

The close relationship between unilateral power and death is revealed the moment three things are recognized. First, the manipulation of the external world is best accomplished if the external world is made up of objects to be manipulated. If entities that make up the external world have "minds of their own," the task of moving the external world without being moved oneself is complicated; hence, living beings must in some sense become objects if unilateral power is going to be successful. Second, when a living entity becomes an object, it is dead. Third, living entities must either be killed or treated as if they are dead when unilateral power is exercised.

Unilateral power does not actually need to kill to be effective. Living entities often cooperate with unilateral power and act as if they are dead. Most of the time, such cooperation is the result of the unadulterated threat of death. People cooperate because they are afraid that they will be killed if they do not. Other, people cooperate with unilateral power because they think they benefit from such cooperation. In other words, they prefer a metaphorical death to the real thing. Certain employer/employee relationships are illustrative. It is not unusual for employees to obey a memo stating that the boss wants them in a meeting even though they know that the meeting is a waste of time. When they cooperate without question, they make themselves into objects. They move their bodies into the meeting room like furniture movers move tables and chairs. They treat their bodies as if they were dead. The employees cooperate with unilateral power because unilateral power confers certain benefits. In a job setting, these benefits include money, health care and pensions. The workers cooperate because they believe that they need these things to live. The dominator system would have them believe that they have no alternative.

Jesus opposed unilateral power. The Gospel of John says that on the night before his crucifixion Jesus washed his disciple's feet (Jn. 13). In other words, one of Jesus' last acts was to reverse the roles of master and disciple. Unilateral power demands that masters be ranked above their disciples. If anyone's feet were to be washed, it would be the disciple who washed the master's feet.

After washing his disciples' feet, Jesus interprets this act saying, "You call me Teacher and Lord; and you are right, for so I am. If I then, your Lord and teacher, have washed your feet, you also ought to wash one another's feet" (Jn. 13: 13, 14). In other words, Jesus' disciples are to serve. They are not to be served. The way of service is not the way of unilateral power. Those who employ unilateral power are served by others. They do not serve others.

Similarly, in Mark 10: 35-45 James and John ask Jesus if they can sit one on his right hand and one on his left when Jesus comes to his glory. Jesus says that such a request is beyond his power to grant. When the rest of the disciples hear of their request, they get angry with James and John. They probably are angry because James and John "beat them to the punch" and asked Jesus the same question they wanted to ask.

> And when the ten heard it, they began to be indignant at James and John. And Jesus called them to him and said to them, "You know that those who are supposed to rule over the Gentiles lord it over them, and their great men exercise authority over them. But it shall not be so among you; but whoever would be great among you must be your servant, and whoever would be first among you must be slave of all. For the Son of man also came not to be served but to serve, and to give his life as a ransom for many." (Mk. 10: 41-45).

Unilateral power is rejected. This rejection applies to Jesus and to Jesus' disciples and followers. It is impossible for someone to follow Jesus and use unilateral power. Jesus came to serve. His mission is the opposite of unilateral power.

Jesus refuses to use unilateral power because of its relationship to death. Jesus' power is the power of life we have called communal power. Communal power is the power employed by partnership ways. Communal power is often confused with something people now call "power with" or "power together," but such phrases do no adequately reflect the sort of power Jesus employed. This is the case because the leaders of Nazi Germany could in some sense be described as employing "power with" or "power together." Communal power is not known so much for how many people use it together. Communal power is known for how it affects those who use it and those who receive it.

In his book *the Social Teaching of the Black Churches*, Peter Paris describes communal power as the capacity to influence others while at the same time being influenced by others. Communal power is a force that recognizes the primacy of community to promote and enrich the world.[15] Communal power is not passive. It is a power that resides in the community. It is a power of the community to change itself, its members and the world at-large.[16] An important example of communal power is the American Civil Rights movement.

> C. Eric Lincoln argues that the decisive dif-
> ference between the Montgomery bus boycott and
> the history of black churches is that the black reli-
> gious leaders for the first time challenged the
> white establishment over something specific, in
> which one side or the other had to emerge as vic-
> tor. The victory that blacks achieved in that event
> was unprecedented, and it changed the whole his-
> tory of the black struggle for racial justice to say
> nothing of the psychological impact on all who
> participated directly or indirectly. That type of
> activity enabled blacks to become initiators of
> action rather than respondents. In that event, we
> see black religious leaders utilizing communal
> power in its full sense, that is, aiming at producing
> an effect and undergoing an effect and both in the
> interest of enhancing community.[17]

The civil rights movement reveals several aspects of communal power. First, it is not passive. It might be best described as non-violent, but it is not passive. It produces an effect. Second, communal power is different from unilateral power in that its effect is not in one direction. It does not originate from an unmoved center against a world of objects. Those who use communal power both produce an effect and undergo an effect. Those who exercise communal power will be changed along with those they seek to change. Third, communal power involves making an adjustment based upon what the external world is communicating. Communal power is like a dance where those who use it respond to the movements of the other. They become like dance partners who end up in a different place than the one at which they began the dance. Moreover, they may have had fun getting there!

Jesus' crucifixion embodies the conflict between unilateral and communal power. Accordingly, it was a struggle between the dominator system and partnership ways. The political and religious leaders, who are always the upper crust of the dominator system, conspired to do away with Jesus. In the Gospels of Matthew, Mark and Luke, these leaders were given their excuse to kill Jesus when Jesus cleansed the Temple, however, the Gospel of John may be telling the true theological story when it says that the act that led to the decision to execute Jesus was Jesus raising Lazarus from the dead (Jn. 11: 47-53).

Just how raising someone from the dead could possibly be a threat of such magnitude is lost on us unless we recognize that a conflict between the dominator system and partnership ways is taking place in Jesus' ministry. Whereas the partnership ways use communal power to support, sustain and enrich life, the dominator system maintains itself by the use of unilateral power. The threat of death lurks behind all manifestations of unilateral power. Those the dominator system cannot assimilate, it seeks to isolate and destroy. In raising Lazarus from the grave (Jn. 11), Jesus was challenging the very power that supports the dominator system. The dominator system's death threat means nothing if the dead do not remain dead. If the dead can rise up and walk out of their tombs, the dominator system loses its power because the threat of death is undermined. This is why the leadership thought they had to kill Jesus when he raised Lazarus from the tomb. Their status (rank) depended on the dead remaining dead. They could not have someone running around raising the dead. Despite their differences, they organized to execute Jesus.

The struggle between the dominator system and partner-ship ways continued after Jesus was arrested. Jesus refused to use unilateral power in the course of this struggle. To do so would have meant that he had succumbed to the dominator system. He told his disciples to put away their swords and not to defend him (Jn. 18: 19-21). Moreover, if Jesus is actually the Son of God as Christians claim, Jesus had legions of angels at his disposal. He could have used them to destroy those who wanted to kill him. He did not raise a hand. He did not employ the power of death even in

111

self-defense. Finally, when Jesus told Pilate, his Roman judge, that his rule was not "of this world," he probably meant that his rule did not employ the same tactics as that of the world's leaders (Jn. 18: 36). He was not a ruler in the dominator system. His rule was a different way. His rule was more consistent with life.

Saying that Jesus did not fight the adherents of the dominator system with their own tactics is not the same as saying that Jesus did not fight. He fought. He resisted the dominator system, but he employed some weapons of the partnership way. He forgave his executioners (Lk. 23: 34). *To those of us who are under the influence of the dominator system, forgiveness does not seem like much of a weapon. In fact, it is a weapon against the dominator system. It is not a weapon that takes life. It is a weapon that gives life.* One need only note how many human relationships die because forgiveness does not happen, and how many live because forgiveness has been bestowed to recognize the profound relationship between forgiveness and the power of life. *Forgiveness is not forgetting. Forgiveness is refusing to insist on one's rights.* This is a very difficult thing to do within the dominator system because one's rights are usually synonymous with one's rank. Forgiveness, therefore, does not happen too much within the dominator system, but, when it happens within the dominator system, life is given. When a criminal is pardoned, life is restored. Forgiveness keeps life connected, and these connections enhance and sustain all in the web of life.

As its name implies, communal power is lodged in community. This is why the creation of communities that are an alternative to the dominant culture is so important in the Bible. Jesus himself began such a community from the cross. He looked at the disciple whom he loved and his mother Mary and said to his disciple, "Behold your mother," and to his mother, "Behold your son" (Jn. 19: 26, 27). We have seen the importance of alternative communities in the Old Testament as well. Jethro tried to create an alternative community based upon judges that employed communal power rather than unilateral power. In his dying moments Jesus recognized this need as well. The early followers of Jesus created a number of new communities in their attempt to live in the Spirit of Jesus. The sort of power that is used by such communities is communal power.

From beginning to end, Jesus' life was in conflict with the dominator system. In his teaching, preaching, healing, miracles, table fellowship, choice of friends and crucifixion, he displayed an alternative way of life. He called this alternative the rule of God. His was probably one of many partnership ways that are open to all, but seen by few.

Chapter 6:

Living in the Spirit of Jesus

Jesus of Nazareth was more influential after he died than any other human being. His influence spread because his followers proclaimed that Jesus rose from the grave. Jesus' followers did not think that the risen Jesus was merely a resuscitated corpse. A resuscitated corpse may have "dodged a bullet," but death still is in its future. Jesus' followers believed that Jesus was resurrected from the dead. Death was behind him. No longer did Jesus have to face death.

In the context of the dominator system, Jesus' resurrection demonstrates that Jesus was no longer under the dominator system's control. Jesus' followers believed that the powers of the dominator system had done their work on Jesus. The dominator system had killed him. Yet, Jesus was alive! Jesus lived with death behind him. Since the power of death was the only power behind the dominator system, the dominator system no longer had power over Jesus. Moreover, since the followers of Jesus thought that their destiny was linked to Jesus' destiny, they believed that the dominator system had no power over them as well. Jesus' followers did not simply teach about Jesus. Many accepted death at the hands of the dominator system rather than deny this link between Jesus' resurrection and their own destinies. Through Jesus' victory over the dominator system, they too had been liberated from its dominion. Apparently such testimony was quite compelling. Christianity spread.

Paul's Conversion

The Apostle Paul was most responsible for the spread of the word about Jesus. That Paul would be such a person is surprising because Paul never was a disciple of Jesus. He was not one of the twelve. Indeed, while the disciples were following Jesus, Paul was learning how to be a good Pharisaic Jew. While the very early Christians were being persecuted, Paul was doing the persecuting. While Stephen, the first Christian martyr, was being stoned to death, Paul was holding the cloaks of those crushing Stephen with rocks (Acts 7: 58).

All Paul knew about Jesus was that Jesus was crucified. This fact alone was enough to condemn Jesus. Every Pharisaic Jew knew that the crucifixion meant that Jesus died cursed by God. The Torah (also called the Law of Moses, or the Law or the first five books of the Bible) said,

> And if a man has committed a crime punishable by death and he is put to death, and you hang him on a tree, his body shall not remain all night upon the tree, but you shall bury him the same day, for a hanged man is accursed by god; you shall not defile your land which the Lord your God gives you for an inheritance. (Dt. 21: 22, 23).

According to the Torah, Jesus died cursed by God. He died on the wrong side of the line that separates the worthy from the unworthy, the saints from the sinners, the clean from the unclean, the godly from the ungodly and the blessed from the cursed.

Paul was scandalized by the fact that Jesus' disciples were claiming that Jesus was the Messiah of Israel. How could the Messiah die cursed by God? Paul knew that those who proclaimed this Jesus as the Messiah were blasphemers. He thought they were insane. The Torah said this clearly and unambiguously. The one convicted of a crime punishable by death (as Jesus clearly was) and hung on a tree (as Paul thought the cross to be) was under God's curse. In accord with the mentality of the dominator system, Paul believed that Jesus' followers had to be stopped even if it meant a few people had to die. Thus, Paul assisted in the stoning of Stephen. He then was commissioned to go to Damascus to help blot out this dangerous blasphemy in that great city. Paul, however, drastically changed on the way to Damascus. He said that he encountered the *crucified* and risen Jesus on that road. Everything changed.

Paul's alleged encounter with the crucified Messiah created one of the most profound and far reaching intellectual dilemmas in the history of religion. Paul clearly believed that he had encountered the crucified and risen Jesus. He was convinced that Jesus was the Messiah of Israel as a result. He also knew that the Torah cursed someone who was crucified. *In short, Paul believed that the <u>Messiah</u> of God died <u>cursed</u> by God according to the <u>Law</u> (Torah) of God.*[1] To put it mildly, Paul had to make certain intellectual adjustments. To say it more forcefully, in Paul's writings (Romans, I and II Corinthians, Galatians, Philippians, I and II Thessalonians, Philemon, and perhaps Ephesians and Colossians), we encounter the first repentant mind in Christian history.

Paul's repentant mind led him to reinterpret the Torah. This did not entail a mere reinterpretation of select verses. It meant a paradigm shift. Paul had to change his thinking about the way the Torah as a whole should be understood. Paul's former, Pharisaic way of understanding the Torah was ruled out from the start. This interpretation used the Law of Moses (Torah) to separate the good and righteous ones from the bad and unrighteous ones. It was thought that the purpose of the Torah was to put a person on the righteous path and help someone better understand the requirements of righteousness.

Paul's conversion experience contradicted this view of the Torah. According to the Torah, Jesus was not worthy of salvation because he had died cursed by God. He was not righteous. The Torah could not have been more clear about the fact that Jesus died on the wrong side of the line separating the worthy from the unworthy. If Jesus was the Messiah, Pharisaic interpretations of the Torah were wrong. For the Torah to have any value for Christians, a different way of interpreting it had to be developed.

Had we been in Paul's position, we might have completely rejected the validity of the Torah altogether. If Jesus is the Messiah, and the Torah curses the Messiah, then that may simply prove that the Law of Moses is invalid. Indeed, Paul comes close to doing this in the seventh chapter of his letter to the Romans.

> Do you not know...that the Law is binding on a person only during his life? Thus a married woman is bound by Law to her husband as long as he lives; but if her husband dies she is discharged from the Law concerning the husband. Accordingly, she will be called an adulteress if she lives with another man while her husband is alive. But

if her husband dies she is free form that law, and
if she marries another man she is not an adulter-
ess.

Likewise…you have died to the Law through
the body of Christ, so that you may belong to another, to him who has been raised from the dead
in order that we may bear fruit for God. While we
were living in the flesh, our sinful passions,
aroused by the Law, were at work in our members
to bear fruit for death. But now we are discharged
from the Law, dead to that which held us captive,
so that we serve not under the old written code but
in the new life of the Spirit. (Rom. 7: 1-6).

According to Paul, the Law (Torah) still exists, and, while
it may still have its purpose or function, Jesus' followers are
"discharged from the Law" because they have died to the Law
through the body of Christ. The Law of Moses might still delineate
the righteous from the unrighteous for those who choose to be
under the Law, but the followers of Jesus have been discharged
from the Law.

In the first three chapters of Romans, Paul addresses the
ability of the Torah (Law of Moses) to draw the moral divide. He
argues that the Gentiles (non-Jews) of the world should know the
Law of God simply through observation of God's creation.
Consequently, Gentiles have no excuse when they do not follow
what they clearly see (Rom. 1: 18-20.) The Jews were explicitly
given the Law of Moses; however, what they do with the Law is
itself a violation of the Law. According to Paul, they think that the
allegiance they show to the Torah makes them examples for all to
imitate. This breaks the Law because, in making themselves
examples, they substitute themselves for God. They are, therefore,
engaged in idolatry (Rom. 2: 17-24). Since all human beings are
either Jew or Gentile, and since Paul has shown that both the Jews
and Gentiles fall far short of what the Law (Torah) requires, Paul
concludes that the Law of Moses does not make anyone righteous:

None is righteous, no not one;

No one understands, no one seeks for God.

All have turned aside, together they have gone
wrong;

No one does good,

Not even one (Rom 3: 10-12).

In other words, if the Torah draws the line separating the righteous from the unrighteous, everyone is on the wrong side of the line.

Paul's conclusion that no one is righteous if measured by the Law of Moses, hints at one way Paul attempts to reinterpret the Law of Moses. If the Law of Moses is still useful, Paul had to admit that it does not separate the righteous from the unrighteous. Accordingly, it cannot disclose what we must do in order to make ourselves righteous. Instead, the Law reveals the true depth of our plight. It reveals that righteousness is out of our reach. There is nothing we can do to make ourselves good, right or just. According to Paul, one function of the Law of Moses (Torah) is to reveal this to us.

If Paul is correct, something very subtle but very important has happened. A wedge has been driven between religion and morality. Under the dominator system, morality always finds an ally in religion. Religion justifies morality. It gives divine sanction to morality's separation of the good from the bad, the worthy from the unworthy and the righteous from the unrighteous. If, however, the purpose of the Law of Moses is to reveal that no one is or will ever be "righteous," then there can be no line separating the righteous from the unrighteous. This liberates religion from the dominator system because religion no longer functions in the ranking process.

The Failure to Convert Christianity

Despite Paul's influence, Christianity failed to free itself from the dominator system and continued to think with the dominator paradigm. In driving a wedge between religion and morality, Paul was on the verge of developing a spirituality that was independent of the dominator system. Heretofore, spirituality concerned what must be done to attain some kind of righteousness or salvation. Accordingly, people could be divided and ranked according to their level of spiritual achievement. Paul, however, denied that there could be such achievement. He believed that no one was righteous before the Law of Moses, and that God granted righteousness as a gift. (Rom. 4: 1-5; Gal. 3: 6).

The dominator system, however, is quite resilient. It is capable of interpreting almost anything within its paradigm, and Paul's theology was not an exception. Adherents of the dominator system reinterpreted Paul in two ways. On the one hand, it agreed with Paul's statement that "no one is righteous" according to the Law of Moses (Torah). It acknowledged that people could never achieve the perfection that the Law of Moses required; however, it asserted that people should at least try. If people just tried to act in accord with the Law, Jesus stood ready to give everyone the grace needed to close the gap between their insufficient efforts and the perfection the Law of Moses intended. While no one could possibly do what the Law of Moses required, dominator thinking asserted that some people could get closer to this standard than others. Those whose spiritual discipline allowed them to come closer to the high standards of the Law of Moses were ranked above those who could not achieve such heights. Christians could still keep the line separating the good from the bad. Ranking still functioned. The dominator model remained intact.

Not all Christians were satisfied with this understanding because they did not think it was faithful to Paul's radical understanding. Echoing Paul, they believed that no action could bring us closer to the perfection that the Law of Moses required. The gap was insurmountable. The dominator system could even incorporate this radical view into its scheme. It acknowledged the contention that there is nothing that we can do to even approach meriting God's grace. It also acknowledged that God alone could grant salvation and that this was done purely through grace. It then went on to say that before all time God chose to save some human beings and to damn others. The line between the saved and the damned had been maintained. It was now drawn by God and not by the righteous actions, thoughts or beliefs of human beings. *The dominator system, you see, does not care who draws the line. The dominator system only cares that the line is drawn.* Once drawn, the line assists in ranking – the process essential to the dominator system.[2]

In general, Christian theology has tried to interpret Paul without abandoning the dominator paradigm, and the wedge between religion and ranking that Paul was trying to achieve no longer exists within Christianity. *Nearly every theological debate that has occurred within the Church is a consequence of the fact that we are attempting to discuss love, grace and life within the dominator paradigm, and the dominator paradigm has no place for love, grace and life.* As long as Christians use the dominator paradigm, Jesus, Paul and the Bible itself will be unintelligible. We will be like geologists attempting to understand the earth with an intellectual paradigm that maintains that the earth is 6000 years old. As accurate geological study is impossible under such a paradigm, so is faithful Christian theology impossible using the dominator system's intellectual paradigm.

The Torah under the Partnership Paradigm

When the dominator system's intellectual paradigm is not employed, Paul's contention that no one is righteous under the Law may say more about the Law of Moses (Torah) than it does about human beings. According to Paul, the Law of Moses has been used improperly. It was never intended to be a standard. The Law was not supposed to be a way to salvation. It was designed for other purposes.

Most New Testament writers try to interpret the Law of Moses apart from the dominator paradigm. Paul's contention that the Law was created to reveal the depth of our sin is an example that has already been discussed, but this was not his only attempt to address this issue. In his letter to the Galatians, Paul understands the Law of Moses to be like a schoolmaster or disciplinarian (PAIDAGOGOS). The theory Paul suggests is that before Christ, the Law was necessary in order to instruct and discipline; however, just as a student graduates and no longer needs his or her teacher, we do not need the discipline of the Law after Jesus. Even James, who is often considered to be the opposite of Paul, tries to free the Law of Moses from the dominator paradigm. Following admonitions against the dominator system's habit of granting rich people higher rank and esteem than poor people, James counsels his readers to speak and act as people who will be judged by the law of liberty. He says that people cannot expect to be treated mercifully if they do not treat others mercifully, but that merciful behavior triumphs over judgment every time (Js. 2: 1 – 13).

The 10th chapter of Mark offers another way to interpret the Law of Moses using the partnership paradigm. Here some Pharisees ask Jesus if the Law of Moses allows a man to divorce his wife. In typical fashion, Jesus asks them to tell him what the Law says. The Pharisees tell him that the Law of Moses says that a man can write a certificate of divorce and send his wife away. Here Jesus' questioners are referring to Deuteronomy 24 where it says, "Suppose a man marries a woman and later decides that he does not want her because he finds something about her he does not like. So he writes her a certificate of divorce and sends her out of his house" (Deut. 24: 1).

Jesus response is interesting. He tells his questioners that Moses wrote this law "for your hardness of heart" (Mk. 10: 5). This response would have caught the questioning Pharisees by surprise. The Pharisees thought that the Law was given in order to justify, and they thought this particular section from the Law of Moses justified men when they divorced their wives. In short, they thought that the Law of Moses gave a man a righteous way out of a marriage. He could write a certificate, and all would be well with his soul. Jesus tells them that there is no justification for divorce saying, "For this reason, man shall leave his father and mother and be joined to his wife, and the two shall become one flesh. What therefore God has joined together, let not man put asunder" (Mk. 10: 7-9). Jesus' response presents an interesting anomaly to those who think that the purpose of the Law of Moses is to justify the ones who practice it. *Jesus never says that it is unlawful for a man to divorce his wife.* The Law of Moses in fact says it is lawful, and Jesus does not deny this. *What Jesus does say is that there is no justification for divorce. In other words, it is possible to follow the letter of the Mosaic Law and not be justified.* At least with respect to divorce, Mosaic Law is for our "hardness of heart." It is not for our justification.

One can only speculate as to what Jesus may have meant when he said that this law is for your hardness of heart. What is pretty clear is that the culture from which this law came was patriarchal to an extreme no longer realized in the Western world. Women were considered property in Jesus' day. The vast majority of women could survive only through their attachment to a man. Furthermore, a man viewed another man's wife as property. He could not take another man's wife without suffering a severe penalty (the woman would suffer a greater penalty). Accordingly, a man could not risk simply taking a seemingly unattached woman to be his wife. He could not risk the penalty he would incur even if he were to do so unknowingly. The only hope a woman had of getting married again would be to show her divorce certificate. Her mere word would not be accepted. Her survival depended on her having this certificate. In a small but important way, the certificate of divorce protected the woman. It was not a justification for the man's behavior. The certificate of divorce offered the divorced woman some sort of safety net within an oppressive patriarchal social structure. It was not much, but it was something.

In responding to questions about divorce, Jesus interprets the Law outside the dominator paradigm. Jesus believed that divorce violated God's plan, yet, divorce was allowed by the Law. To put it simplistically, the divorce law is a law that recognizes that human beings are going to disregard divine plans. It answers the question what should be done when we violate God's plans.[3] In this day and age, we view the purpose of our laws differently. When something happens that we do not like, we write a law against it, and punish those who violate the law. For example, our drug laws punish drug possession and use. They do not cover what we as a society might do when someone violates the drug laws. Hence, people do not get the help they need with their drug dependencies, and most of our prison inmates are in prison on drug related charges. These incarcerations cost the nation millions of dollars.

By the same token, human beings will soon be cloning other human beings. Many think that cloning human beings is a violation of God's law or the laws of nature. Accordingly, laws have been written against human cloning. No laws, however, have been written to address what happens when scientists inevitably clone a human being. We should, for example, write laws that give human clones the rights of all human beings. Human clones will not receive rights automatically. Legislation will be required. The U.S. Constitution, for example, did not give African slaves rights, and our laws consider corporations to be persons under the law. A law can give the rights of a person to anything, or a law can deny human beings the rights of a person. Granting human clones the rights of human beings would make things like cloning human beings for their body parts illegal. It would prevent human clones from being denied their humanity.

Mark's interpretation of Mosaic divorce law has other implications as well. It suggests that, under the partnership paradigm, people are more important than the rules.[4] Under the dominator system rules are clearly more important than people. Since Jesus was operating under a partnership paradigm, he upheld the importance of people over rules – even rules as important as Mosaic Law. The Gospels of Matthew, Mark and Luke tell of Jesus' conflict with Sabbath Laws (Mt. 12: 1-8; Mk. 2: 23-28; Lk. 6: 1-5). In all of these instances, Jesus or his disciples did something that the religious authorities considered a violation of Sabbath laws. On all of these occasions, Jesus responded that human beings were not created for the Sabbath. The Sabbath was created to benefit human beings. In other words, people are more important than rules.

The dominator system always holds that the rules are more important than people. It must because the rules maintain the ranking that is essential to the dominator system. Without strict adherence to the rules, the dominator system falls. We are so accustomed to the dominator system that we do not see the destructive side of the belief that rules are more important than people. We fail to understand that the source of much individual calamity is the high esteem in which we hold these man-made rules. Women tolerate abusive relationships because they do not "believe in" divorce, and their friends and counselors often seek to preserve the marriage despite the existence of a life-threatening situation. Men and women often forsake their dreams in favor of careers that deny their spirits because such careers are safer, at least according to the rules by which we are living. A choice like that may not reflect the immediate danger of the woman who refuses to divorce her violent husband, but in the long run it places a person's life in as much jeopardy. Whenever rules are deemed more important than the person, a person's spirit is diminished, and a person's life is threatened.

New Testament Communities

If the Torah is freed from the dominator paradigm, it no longer functions in the service of morality. It does not separate the worthy from the unworthy or the good from the bad. The New Testament writers took this new state of affairs one step further. They noted that when the worthy are not separated from the unworthy, new sorts of communities are created. These communities are different from each other, but they are all alternatives to the dominant culture.

This fact was already demonstrated in our discussion of the Exodus. Immediately following the Exodus from Egypt, the people of Israel attempted to create an alternative community. Unlike the monarchies that surrounded them, the Israelites were a loose confederation of tribes governed by Judges. In the same manner, many of the New Testament writers envision an alternative community. These alternative visions are prompted by the fact that they are no longer thinking within the dominator paradigm. Accordingly, they cannot use rank and status – primary characteristics of the dominator system – in the formulation of their communities.

Before discussing some of these alternative communities in detail, it is important to note that the formation and life within such communities is a topic most New Testament writers discuss. A primary concern of James is how the poor in his church are to be treated. John equates faithfulness to Jesus with loving one's brother or sister in Christ (I John 2: 9 – 11). John of Patmos writes out of concern that the Christian communities of Asia Minor persevere in the midst of oppression from the dominator system. These communities all differ, but they are all alternatives to the dominant culture.

In the third chapter of Paul's letter to the Galatians, Paul demonstrates that relationship between alternative community and understanding the Law of Moses apart from the dominator paradigm. In Galatians 3: 24, Paul reinterprets the purpose of Mosaic Law. "So that the law was our custodian until Christ came, that we might be justified by faith. But now that faith has come, we are no longer under a custodian." Immediately Paul recognizes the social consequences of this reinterpretation of the Law saying, "For as many of you as were baptized into Christ have put on Christ. There is neither Jew nor Greek, there is neither slave nor free, there is neither male nor female; for you are all one in Christ Jesus" (Gal. 3: 26, 27).

Because Mosaic Law does not justify, no lines are drawn that separate the Jew from the non-Jew or the slave from the free or the male from the female. No distinctions are made because these distinctions are drawn only if the Law of Moses is subject to the dominator system. Only when the Law of Moses serves the dominator system does it draw lines that determine a person's worthiness or unworthiness before God. Only when the Law of Moses serves the dominator system does it distinguish between Jew and Gentile, male and female or slave and free. Only when the Law of Moses serves the dominator system does it rationalize the differences between people and make it appear that these rationalizations have divine status.

Paul recognized that if Jesus – the one that Mosaic Law said had died cursed by God – is actually the Messiah of God, Mosaic Law could not serve the dominator system. According to the dominator system's interpretation of Mosaic Law, Jesus had died on the wrong side of the divide. The only way that Paul could make sense of Jesus was to deny that Mosaic Law drew such lines. Moreover, communities that are "in Christ" have no business ranking one person or group above another. To the extent that the communities have done so, they have become slaves to the dominator system and are not faithful to Jesus.

In Paul's first letter to the Corinthians, he discusses the matter a little differently. He interprets Christian community organically rather than hierarchically. He calls the Church the Body of Christ. He proceeds to say that no part of the body is of higher status than another part. According to Paul, the eye of the body needs the hand and the head needs the feet. If one part suffers, all suffer together. If one part is honored, all rejoice (I Cor. 12: 14 – 26). This description of the Christian community is similar to the manner in which partnership ways honor diversity. Diversity is honored because diversity enhances life. Just as a forest needs many species in order to thrive, Paul's Christian community needs diversity in order to be a body. Everything contributes to the life of the whole, and the whole is diminished by the loss or suffering of any of its parts.

Ample evidence testifies to the early Church's efforts to establish communities that were an alternative to the dominator system. Acts 4: 32-35 is an important example:

Now the company of those who believed was of one heart and soul, and no one said that any of the things which he possessed was his own, but they had everything in common. And with great power the apostles gave their testimony to the resurrection of the Lord Jesus, and great grace was upon them all. There was not a needy person among them, for as many as were possessor of lands or houses sold them, and brought the proceeds of what was sold, and laid it at the apostles' feet; and distribution was made to each as any had need. (Acts 4: 32-35).

This was a community were needs were met. People received what was needed, and no one was in want. This is in sharp contrast to communities enslaved to the dominator system. As previously noted, the dominator system received its start when food was made a commodity. This entailed the development of criteria that established whether or not a person was worthy enough to receive food. Those who met the criteria ate. Those who did not meet the criteria starved. A person's need for food was irrelevant. The only thing that was relevant was whether or not the person in question had met the established criteria. In the alternative community that the followers of Jesus tried to construct, a person's need was the determining factor. If a person needed something, he or she received it if the community could provide it. A characteristic of cultures under the dominator system is starvation in the midst of plenty. The early Christian community would have none of this.

Another characteristic of the alternative community that the early followers of Jesus attempted to create can be seen in Matthew 18: 15-20. This passage is actually about an excommunication. At first glance, it might seem rather odd to select a passage concerned with putting someone outside the community as positive evidence for an alternative to the dominant culture, but what is truly important to a group becomes evident when someone is expelled from the group. This passage tells us what is important to early church gatherings.

If your brother sins against you, go and tell him his fault between you and him alone. If he listens to you, you have gained a brother. But if he

126

does not listen, take one or two others along with
you, that every word may be confirmed by the
evidence of two or three witnesses. If he refuses to
listen to them, tell it to the church; and if he refuses to listen even to the church, let him be to
you as a Gentile and a tax collector. (Mt. 18: 15-
18)

This passage gives us much information concerning the
character of the community that the followers of Jesus wished to
establish. The first thing to note is the treatment accorded the one
who is put outside the community. A superficial glance would lead
one to believe that this person is to be treated similarly to the way
that anyone who is expelled from a group is treated. That person is
shunned. Closer examination, however, indicates that this may not
actually be what is happening in this instance.

The statement that the excommunicated one should be
treated as a Gentile or tax collector may be ironic. It is made in
Matthew the tax collector's Gospel. In ancient Palestine, tax
collectors were shunned by their community. They were
considered unworthy for two reasons. As tax collectors, they were
working for the Roman occupiers. They were collaborators with
the enemy. Also, the way a tax collector made a living was by
collecting more than was required. The Roman authorities did not
think this illegal. It was a tax collector's job description. A tax
collector would be assigned to collect a certain amount of money.
If he collected more, he could keep it. If less was collected, the tax
collector would have to make up the difference. In any case, what
the Romans understood as an incentive, the Jewish people
considered extortion. They thought tax collectors were
collaborators and extortionists.

Matthew the tax collector did not experience the same rejection from Jesus as he did from his neighbors. Matthew was
called by Jesus when he was sitting at his tax booth. (Mt. 9:9).
Moreover, Matthew knew that Jesus ate with tax collectors and
others deemed outcast by the people of occupied Israel. Unlike his
countrymen, Jesus did not draw the line that separated the worthy
from the unworthy. His grace extended to the tax collectors and
others deemed unworthy. If his followers were to form a
community in Jesus' spirit, it would have to treat tax collectors in

the same gracious manner. A community of Jesus followers could not shun outcasts and still follow Jesus.

In the second place, the Gospel of Matthew ends with the apostolic commission. In the last paragraph of Matthew, Jesus appears to his disciples and gives them their mission to go and make disciples of all nations. "Baptizing them in the name of the Father and of the Son and of the Holy Spirit, and teaching them all I have commanded you" (Mt. 28: 19, 20). Here the disciples receive their reason for being. They are to go to those who are not a part of the community and teach them. Hence, the one who is set outside the community is not shunned. That person becomes one of the reasons for this community's existence.

Even more is revealed about this community when the reason for the person's dismissal is analyzed. The "brother" is not expelled from the community because of the "sin" he committed. He is dismissed because he did not listen. He did not listen to the one who thinks a sin has been committed. He refused to listen when two others are brought along to hear the complaint, and finally, he does not listen to the church itself. The passage never mentions the nature of the initial sin or grievance. What appears to be important is listening, and it is the brother's refusal to listen that leads to his dismissal.

Since listening is a vital component of the community that the early followers of Jesus were trying to establish, it is imperative to have some understanding of what constitutes listening. In the first place, listening is not simply being in the room when someone else is speaking. It is probably not even the ability to repeat what was said. The brother who refused to listen definitely was in the same room with the offended one, and he probably could have repeated what was said to him. By the same token, listening is not necessarily doing what someone tells you to do or agreeing with what was said. You can disagree and still listen.

Listening involves making an adjustment on the basis of what has been said and heard. After listening, something in your life will be different. Making an adjustment on the basis of what has been heard can involve something very small or something quite profound. An adjustment may merely involve avoiding the use of a particular word because you have found that that word creates an emotional reaction in the person with whom you are speaking. On the other hand, listening may lead you to recognize the depth of your offense, to ask forgiveness and amend your ways. In either case, listening involves making an adjustment on the basis of what the other has said. Finally, the adjustment need not be what the other had in mind for listening to occur, however, the adjustment should be obvious to the other for listening to be effective.

A final surprise concerning listening is revealed when one asks, "Who is more likely to be the person who does not listen?" On a superficial level, the answer is that the one who is most likely not to listen is the one who does not want to change or make an adjustment. This suggestion leads to the more profound contention that the one who does not want to make an adjustment is usually the one with the most to lose. Included in this group are the rich, the powerful and the educated. For example, it is unlikely that one can change an educated person's mind about the things in which he or she is most educated. A person with a Ph.D. in theology is not likely to change his or her mind about some doctrinal matter if challenged by a child in a Sunday School class. This is not to say that the child could not be correct or insightful. It is just to say that the one with a Ph.D. has devoted too much time and invested too much effort to change an opinion on the basis of what a child says. It is also not to say that such a change is impossible. It is just not likely.

The same comments that were just made about the educated also apply to the rich and powerful. Riches or power are at risk when adjustments are made. Thus, the rich and powerful are less likely to listen. It is not that they cannot listen. They are simply less likely to do so. They have too much to protect. By the same token, the powerless, poor and uneducated might be more likely to make adjustments on the basis of what they have heard. This is not to say that they always do. It is simply saying that they are more likely to make adjustments than are the rich, powerful and educated.

In the history of the Church, there are numerous instances of leaders who do not listen because they think they have their position, power, education and riches to protect. The more these men and (few) women are subject to the dominator paradigm, the less likely they will be to listen because their power, riches, position and education are the reasons for their rank. Under the dominator system, one's rank must be protected.

Listening also involves the use of communal power instead of unilateral power. As has been discussed, communal power is the capacity to influence others while being influenced by others.[5] In other words, people make adjustments in their lives whenever they use communal power. Since listening also involves making such adjustments, its relationship to communal power is established.

A community that understands listening to be the most fundamental way its members interact must employ communal power. That the early Church understood listening and communal power to be essential should not be a surprise. Jesus used communal power. Indeed, Jesus refused to use unilateral power because unilateral power is grounded in death. Thus, any community that is in Jesus' spirit must abandon unilateral power in favor of communal power. Paul envisioned a community where there is no distinction between male and female, slave and free or Jew and Gentile (Gal. 3: 28). Luke tells us of an early Christian community where those who participated held all things in common and where each person received what was needed (Acts 4: 32-35). Matthew speaks of a community that understood listening to be its identifying feature (Mt. 18: 15-20).

What is a surprise is how quickly the church became an agent of the dominator system despite the example of Jesus. It rapidly excluded women from positions of leadership. It established a male hierarchy that placed all power and knowledge within its priests and bishops.[6] It developed moralities that justified the established order and drew lines to separate the good from the bad, the worthy from the unworthy, the saved from the damned and the saints from the sinners. It persecuted, tortured and killed its opponents. For a time, it was the most potent force of domination in Western Europe, and even today it longs for the restoration of its former power. It forgets that the power it desires is the same sort of power that killed the one it still calls Lord and Savior.

As has always been the case with Israel, however, there have always been people who oppose the Church's preference for the dominator system. According to Elaine Pagels, the so-called

Gnostic heretics opposed the emerging hierarchy of the "orthodox" churches by denying its claim that truth was the sole property of the bishops and popes.[7] This denial was echoed throughout the centuries by "heretics" whose doctrinal beliefs differed considerably but were united in the belief that the hierarchical church was not the only source of truth and salvation. Even some people the Church now calls saints fell under the scrutiny of heresy hunters in their lifetimes. St. Francis and St. Thomas, for example, received such scrutiny because their practices and teachings implied that the hierarchical Church was not the sole source of divine truth and grace. Because the Christian Church had become subjected to the dominator system, it simply could not tolerate the slightest threat to its dominant position. Accordingly, the church proclaimed that it alone was the source of salvation and truth. No other ways were tolerated. People who disagreed lost their lives. It is now time for the church to abandon its allegiance to the dominator system. Doing so might restore faithfulness to its Lord.

Chapter 7:

Resisting the Dominator System

The Bible is the most ancient literary record of the battle between partnership ways and the dominator system, and it cannot be adequately understood apart from this forgotten struggle. For this reason alone, it is an important document. Like most records, however, it is not an unambiguous account. Many Biblical authors wrote under the influence of the dominator system, and others, like the prophets, clearly served partnership ways.

We have seen, for example, that King Solomon's public relations staff changed the God who liberated the Israelites from Egyptian slavery into a God who actually sanctioned Solomon's enslavement of the Israelites once again. The only difference between the Pharaoh and King Solomon was their respective building projects. Whereas Pharaoh used Israelite slaves to build pyramids, King Solomon used them to build his own palace and "The Temple of the Lord." The irony (as well as the propaganda coup) is that Solomon called his God by the same name that Moses employed. Today it is popular to ask if the warring Christians, Muslims and Jews worship the same God. A more profound Biblical question might be, "Did Moses and Solomon worship the same God?" After all, Moses' God clearly supported partnership ways and opposed the dominator system. Solomon's God supported Israel's version of the dominator system, namely, Israel's monarchy. This conflict between Moses' and Solomon's understanding of God exists throughout Scripture.

This book has argued that the God of the Bible sides with partnership ways, and that the myriad of tensions between partnership ways and the dominator system are present within the Bible because the dominator system was never purged from Israel or Christianity. Several reasons for the belief that the God of the Bible sides with partnership ways have been discussed. First, the Exodus is the most definitive event in the Old Testament. This was an unambiguous challenge to Egypt's version of the dominator system. Israel was created by this event, and the Bible would not exist without Israel. Second, Israel made a conscious attempt to be different from other nations after it was emancipated from Egyptian slavery. Third, prophets who spoke against the path Israel and Judah were taking emerged only when Israel anointed its kings. Prior to the monarchy, no distinction was made between political leadership and prophecy. Moses, Joshua and all of the judges were both political leaders as well as prophets. When the monarchy came into existence, prophets were distinguished from political leadership. Their role was to proclaim alternatives to the monarchy's one dimensional view of life. These prophetic alternatives maintained the tension between the dominator system and partnership ways throughout the Bible.

Over the years, Israel *probably* has been more faithful to the dominator system than partnership ways, but Christianity *certainly* has been more faithful to the dominator system than to Jesus. In his discussion of the emergence of medieval civilization, famed medieval historian Norman Cantor clearly recognizes this fact.

> In the ancient world, in Egypt and Mesopotamia, the social structure was justified on religious grounds. It was God's plan for the world – God's will – and acceptance of the social forms was a religious duty. Medieval men inherited that attitude and built upon it. They had more difficulty than the Egyptians in doing so, however, *because certain strains within Christianity were incompatible with the ancient system. There is an egalitarian strain in the Bible . . . , for example, that runs counter to the ancient traditions of exploitation and domination. Medieval people had to relate these two traditions, and they came out heavily . . . on the side of the ancient, class-dominated, authoritarian society.*[1]

Cantor speaks of the power that the dominator system held over Christianity. Jesus' own disciples fell under its influence (Mk. 10: 35-45), but nearly all of Christianity succumbed to the dominator system's spell by Constantine's reign in the early fourth century. As is the case with Israel, the dominator system's control has never been absolute within Christianity. There have always been Christians who supported partnership ways, but they are usually marginalized in their lifetimes and sanctified in their deaths.

The task before us is to remember the Bible's preference for partnership ways and to resist the dominator system. In the process of our resistance, we might create a few alternatives to the dominant system. Remembrance and resistance can be dangerous, but, in remembering the Biblical God's opposition to the dominator system, we acquire the responsibility to suggest ways to resist the dominator system and to create our own versions of partnership.

This is not the same as saying that we should all go back to some prehistoric past where human beings wandered the planet in small tribes in search of food. Not only is this impossible, it is undesirable at least from my point of view. Speaking personally, I like air conditioning, modern modes of transportation, computers, and, above all, flush toilets. The task before us is much the same as the task facing the Israelites following the Exodus and the early Church following Jesus' death. They did not try to go back to the prehistoric past. They developed their own alternatives to the dominant culture. This is our task as well. It is not so much that the dominator system is the wrong way to live. The problem with the dominator system is that it does not allow alternative ways of life.

The rest of this chapter discusses ways both to resist the dominator system and to create communal relationships that are an alternative to the dominator system. Most of these suggestions have been gleaned from this discussion of the Bible. They are not intended to imply that the Bible is the only resource for such alternatives. Alternatives to the dominator system have occurred throughout the world, and there are many ways to resist. For example, most Native American tribes were alternatives to the dominator system, and these tribes may have been more successful in their resistance than the 12 tribes of Israel were. What follows are forms of resistance that have been gleaned from this discussion of the Biblical narrative. These include: ethical resistance that abandons morality, intellectual resistance that recognizes the contextual nature of truth, spiritual resistance that abandons self-justification for confession, and communal resistance that abandons unilateral power in favor of communal power.

Ethical Resistance

The abandonment of morality is the most important step in the ethical resistance of the dominator system. Abandoning morality is hardly the same as the abandonment of our concern for behavior. Morality is abandoned out of concern for behavior. Morality is linked to death. It is the way the dominator system draws the line between the good and the bad. We have seen that different cultures will draw this moral line in different places because moral criteria and, consequently, moral content differ from culture to culture. We have also noted that while the *content* of morality differs from culture to culture, morality's *function* is forever the same. It always separates "the good" from "the bad."

The dominator system only cares about morality's function. It does not care about morality's content. Different cultures within the dominator system have different moralities. The dominator system only needs a line to be drawn between the good and the bad. It does not care why the line is drawn. Morality exists only where this line is drawn. Where this line is not drawn, morality does not exist. Abandoning morality is the same as the refusal to draw a moral divide separating the good from the bad.

Resisting the dominator system entails the abandonment of morality because morality is the first step in ranking. Ranking, one must remember, is the defining characteristic of the dominator system. Where ranking exists, the dominator system exists. Where ranking does not exist, the dominator system has not yet emerged. In developing criteria whereby the worthy ones are distinguished from the unworthy ones, morality initiates the dominator system's ranking process.

There was no great social need to separate the worthy from the unworthy before the agricultural revolution because food was not a commodity. People lived in small groups that generally moved about in search of food. When the group found food, everyone ate. When there was no food to be found, everyone went hungry. Together they feasted. Together they starved. There was never starvation in the midst of plenty. This social arrangement changed when food became a commodity. When food was placed "under lock and key," criteria for food's distribution needed to be developed. These criteria determined who would receive food and how much food each person would receive. Lines had to be drawn between those worthy of food and those who are unworthy of food. This is the origin of morality. Morality helps perpetuate the dominator system's common practice of the poor starving in the midst of abundance. Efforts to abandon morality, therefore, do not entail abandonment of concern for one's behavior or concern for one's fellow living beings. Abandonment of morality concerns the rejection of social arrangements that perpetuate starvation in the midst of plenty and the moral rationalizations for starvation in the midst of plenty.

Morality's association with death is clear. When morality draws the line between good and evil, those who are on the good side of the line often convince themselves that those on the bad side of the line are there for a good, moral reason. Such thinking allows the good people to falsely conclude that they are under no obligation to care for the bad people. They may have some responsibility for the people who suffer and are not deemed bad, but they are justified in their neglect of the bad ones. This is why every conversation we have concerning the poor and homeless becomes a moral conversation. We only help someone in need if we determine that the person is worthy of our aid. If we determine that the unfortunate woman does not deserve her plight, help is possible. One the other hand, if we determine that the unfortunate woman has contributed to her plight, or if she refuses to do something that we think might help her, then we usually refuse to give her assistance. Why should we help a homeless person who refuses shelter? Why should we give money to an unemployed man who just turned down a job? We generally do not help people such as these because they have not conformed to the moral standards that we think make them worthy of our support. The trouble is that when these people are denied all assistance, death is just around the corner, and our moral thinking has given them this death sentence.

We abandon morality when we refuse to abide by moral standards that leave people for dead. From the perspective of those who find themselves on the "good" side of the moral divide, this means that we give people food, clothing, shelter and other necessities of life to people who the dominator system says are undeserving. From the perspective of those who find themselves on the "bad" side of the arbitrary moral divide, this implies the even more difficult task of asserting your worthiness to live in the face of a culture that thinks you are not worthy of life. We abandon morality when we show mercy and live by grace. What it means to live by grace depends on one's context in life.

Living graciously is the next step in our ethical resistance. Grace is not a principle. Grace is an act in which a person is treated lovingly and in discontinuity with his or her past.[2] Grace is the opposite of morality. Morality always treats a person in continuity with his or her past. Morality always asks the question, "What is in a person's past that demonstrates that person's worthiness or unworthiness for a particular benefit (or penalty)?" Grace takes a different approach. It asks the question, "What does this person need?" It then attempts to give what is needed. A person's past has no bearing on whether or not this need is met. If a person is treated graciously, the need will be met regardless of the person's past. The past is, however, considered in determining what is needed and how the need is to be met. One might meet a drug addict's need for food and shelter in a different way than one might help a child with a similar need. In both situations, however, grace demands that the need be met regardless of moral criteria that would conclude otherwise. Living a gracious life is the opposite of living a moral life.[3] Living graciously is part of what it means to abandon morality and to walk in newness of life.

Ethical resistance requires the social and religious acumen to determine who the dominant culture deems immoral and undeserving. Sometimes this is easy. Most of the time, it is difficult. This task is further complicated by the fact that the moral divide usually has religious sanction, and opposing the moral divide is often equated with opposing human decency. Moreover, the moral divide shifts as the criteria we use to establish it changes. Accordingly, those once deemed immoral can become moral, and those deemed moral can become immoral.

It takes a great deal of social and religious awareness to recognize the people or groups a given culture deems immoral. We are often mesmerized by our culture. We tend to count its values as absolute. We adopt our culture's definition of who is bad and who is good. Our uncritical acceptance of our culture's moral dictates does not depend on education level or spirituality. It is a consequence of the difficulty we have of being critical of ourselves and our culture. Many highly educated German Lutherans, for example, supported the Nazi agenda, and many fine

Christian Americans thought the segregation policies of the South were established by God. The habit of uncritically adopting the culture's arbitrary moral standards is not even confined to those who find themselves on the privileged side of the moral divide. Tragically, those who find themselves on the "bad" side of the moral divide are often persuaded that they deserve their fate. The poor are persuaded that they are completely responsible for their poverty. Women have accepted the secondary status assigned to them by patriarchal societies. African Americans once accepted the position assigned to them by their racist culture.

Ethical resistance requires the courage to reject the moral pronouncements of the dominator system. In recent years we have seen this courage expressed by African Americans who refuse to accept the White dominator system's definition of who they ought to be. We have seen it expressed by members of the Polish movement, Solidarity. We have seen this courage lived out in Tiananmen Square. This courage has also been expressed by women in resistance to patriarchy.

Courage is also required if those who find themselves on the "good" side of the moral divide are to resist the dominator system. It takes a certain amount of courage for someone on the "good" side of the moral divide to identify with someone on the "bad" side. People who do so sometimes find their character is called into question. Just as an elementary school student who befriends a socially unacceptable classmate runs the risk of becoming a social outcast, a person who identifies with someone considered immoral risks being considered morally corrupt or even worthy of death by virtue of this association.

It is one thing to say that one person should identify with another. It is another to say what this entails. At the very least, identification involves listening to the other. As has been discussed, listening involves making an adjustment in your life on the basis of what has been communicated. People change because they have listened. Listening to those on the wrong side of the moral divide might allow the listener to understand that some people are deemed immoral because of a social disorder instead of a personal defect. Listening might create realization that many prisoners are prisoners because of race, poverty or unjust laws instead of being threats to society.

Another way to identify with those on the wrong side of the moral divide is to try to tell their stories. We have a tendency to dehumanize those our culture calls immoral because we focus on the rules they have violated rather than on the people they are. Telling the story of such a person or group gives them back their humanity. The simple act of telling such stories makes the people more important than the rules. When a person is understood, it is much more difficult to leave that person for dead.

Providing support is another way to identify with someone. Support can involve prayer, monetary contributions, education, friendship or political action. At some point, support may simply involve giving people a place to assemble and defending their right to gather. As is the case with all forms of identification, these activities are not without personal risk, but they are essential in our resistance of the dominator system.

Jesus is an excellent example of ethical resistance to the dominator system. He abandoned morality. He never answered a moral question. Doing so would have drawn the line between the good ones and the bad ones. If Jesus actually answered moral questions, he would have assisted the dominator system with its ranking process. Any answer he might have given to any moral question would have compelled his followers to create a moral divide. In refusing to give such answers, Jesus deprived adherents of the dominator system of the starting point of the ranking process. Ranking could not begin with Jesus' words on moral subjects because Jesus does not provide such words.

Second, Jesus knew that people were more important than rules. We have discussed Jesus' preference of people over rules in his many controversies surrounding Sabbath regulations (Mt. 12: 1-8; Mt. 12: 9-14; Mk. 2: 23-27; Jn. 9: 14.). On every occasion, Jesus reminds us that the Sabbath laws were made for people. People were not made for the Sabbath. The dominator system is undermined whenever people are thought more important than rules because this attitude prevents the moral rules from being used to rank the people.

Third, Jesus always identified with those on the wrong side of the moral divide. He socialized with prostitutes and tax collectors. He spoke to Samaritan women. He healed the sick and others deemed unclean by certain interpretations of the Torah. At a time in history when men considered contact with children demeaning to their rank, Jesus held children in his arms and blessed them.

Jesus' crucifixion was his ultimate identification with those who were on the wrong side of the moral divide. The Romans understood crucifixion as the supreme form of capital punishment. Often called "the slaves' punishment," the Romans used crucifixion to deter slave rebellion.[4] In other words, Jesus identified with slaves when he was crucified. Rome had no lower rank than slave. Furthermore, we have also seen that Jesus' crucifixion meant that he died cursed by God. The Torah itself stated that one who hung on a tree (as Jesus was thought to have done) had God's curse upon him (Dt 21: 22, 23). Such a person died in a place God could not go. Such a person was incapable of redemption. According to Roman custom, Jesus died a slave's death. According to the Torah, Jesus died as a vile, immoral individual who was cut off and cursed by God Himself.[5] Believers and unbelievers alike must recognize that Jesus' crucifixion means that Jesus' last breath was taken on the immoral side of the line that both Rome and Judaism drew to separate the good from the bad, the clean from the unclean and the saved from the damned.

One final observation illustrates Jesus' ethical resistance and his total rejection of morality. Normally, when people identify with those on the wrong side of the moral divide, they argue that the people with whom they are identifying are good, and their "oppressors" are bad. For example, people who identify with the poor often maintain that the poor are good and the rich are morally corrupt. In doing so, they have not abandoned the moral divide. It remains. It is just that those once deemed good are now deemed bad, and those deemed bad are now thought good. Jesus never fell into this trap. He forgave his executioners. He ate with Pharisees as well as the tax collectors and sinners. *Jesus did not distinguish between good people and bad people. He attacked the moral line itself. Jesus' enemy was the dominator system and the arbitrary distinction it makes between the good and the bad.* Jesus' attack was so radical that the dominator system had to kill him. He was not an enemy of people whose lives were being crushed by the forces of domination. He was not even an enemy of his executioners who were also under the control of the dominator system. He was attacking these forces of control and oppression.

140

Jesus was one of the few people not under the spell of the Tree of the Knowledge of Good and Evil. He was not moral. He attacked all moral divides. He did so in support of the web of life. He did so in support of partnership ways.

Intellectual Resistance

The dominator system proclaims the absurd notion that there is only one way to live, one way to think, one true religion, and one way to organize society.[6] We have seen the ramifications of this view in our discussion of the Pharaoh's hardness of heart. Because of Pharaoh's subjection to the dominator system, he could not let the Hebrew slaves go. He refused to do so despite the havoc their presence heaped on Egyptian culture. He was paralyzed. The one dimensional thinking of the dominator system prevented him from seeing any alternatives. Like Moses, Israel's prophets also presented alternatives to the dominator system, and, like the Pharaoh, those in authority were unable to see any alternative to their single-minded worldview. At the time the prophets made their indictments, their words were largely ignored. Only in retrospect, did the prophets' words get the respect they have come to receive. The words that inaugurated Jesus' ministry called people to repentance. At the very least, repentance means to stop doing what is currently being done and live in a fundamentally different way. That Jesus was killed because of this message indicates that those in the grip of the dominator system cannot even consider repentance because they cannot envision alternatives to their way of life.

The dominator system seeks to reinforce the belief that there is only one way to live by maintaining that there is only one way to think. In our discussion of morality we have seen that individual cultures under the dominator system will regard the competing moral claims of other cultures as evil, misguided or, at best, half truths. The same can be said about competing intellectual claims. If a culture believes that there is one and only one way to live and think, and if that culture encounters another culture making different absolute truth claims, then there is great potential for violence.

This death-dealing potential should be obvious. Osama bin Ladan and George Bush make conflicting truth claims. Both

141

believe their claims are absolutely true. Both think that God is on their side. Both have called alternative claims evil. This, combined with their common belief in a moral divide that separates the good people from the evil people, leads to the tragic belief that God demands the extermination of evil. Ironically, George Bush and Osama bin Ladan hold one belief in common. These sworn enemies also swear allegiance to the dominator system. Their belief that their intellectual and moral positions are absolute places them squarely in the service of the dominator system.

Mentioning George Bush and Osama bin Ladan in this context suggests that this is not a mere intellectual problem. It is a discussion of life and death issues. Since the dominator system tolerates no moral or intellectual alternatives, life is threatened whenever two groups with differing absolutes come into contact. When this occurs, the only alternative a culture under the dominator system has is to strive for absolute dominance. At this point in our history, however, such dominance may be inconsistent with the survival of human life. We can no longer afford the luxury of war because wars now can destroy the planet. Rather than suffer such destruction, we might examine the sources of such destruction. One such source is our intellectual arrogance. Each culture that is subject to the dominator system firmly maintains that its way is the only true way. The world might do well to engage in a philosophical enterprise that reexamines this absurd notion.

Resistance to the dominator system requires an intellectual revolution that rejects absolute claims for truth. This is not the same as saying that we should stop looking for the truth. It is saying that the truth does not assume the form of absolutes. This does not mean that all truth is relative. Indeed, the statement "all truth is relative" is itself an absolute claim. Rather, the claim of partnership ways is that truth is contextual. *In other words, truth always has a context. Truth does not exist without a context.* We have seen how even the truth of the Commandments depend on their context. It is one thing for the God who liberated Israel from Egyptian slavery to say, "You shall not steal." It is quite another for a Southern plantation owner to tell his own slaves these exact words. By the same token, it is one thing to tell a middle aged man to "honor your mother and father." It is something else to say these same words to an eight-year-old girl who is being sexually abused by her parents. The same exact words say different things in different contexts. They are not absolute truths for all times and in all settings.

Claiming that the truth is contextual is not the same as saying that truth does not exist. It is simply saying that *truth exists only in context.* If no relationship exists between one context and another, then the truth of the first context will not apply in the other context. If, on the other hand, one context is similar to another, then the truth of one context may be quite applicable to the other. For example, it has been the argument of this book that much of the Bible's context is similar to ours because the dominator system governs both contexts. Since Moses, the prophets, Jesus and Paul resisted the dominator system their followers should make the same attempt.

Still, to say that truth is contextual is difficult for us to accept. We believe that something is true precisely because it is true forever. We think that if something is not true forever and in all places, it was never true. We feel this way only because of our short attention spans. The fact of the matter is our most cherished scientific truths and moral values have been changed and will continue to change. We simply prefer to ignore this fact and continue to believe that the truth is absolute and unchanging despite the evidence to the contrary. Perhaps this preference for absolutes reflects our subservience to the dominator system. The dominator system needs us to believe that its truths are absolute because its most essential feature is ranking, and ranking depends on the belief in an absolute and unalterable standard of truth. If truth is contextual, then the truths by which we are ranked do not apply in certain contexts. Contextual truth places the dominator system in jeopardy because it undermines the absolute standards by which we rank. We who are subjects of the dominator system have to believe in absolute and unchanging truth because we equate these absolutes with order, and we think we like order.

It is easier for those who are not subject to the dominator system to think differently. In his book, *The Soul of the Indian*, Dr. Charles Eastmann, a famous Sioux physician, narrates an encounter between a Christian missionary and a number of Native Americans from different tribes. The missionary told the people about God creating the world in six days. He told them about the Garden of Eden and about Adam and Eve and the apple. The people listened attentively and thanked the missionary for telling them such a wonderful story. Then one of the listeners told the group his tribe's story about the origin of maize. The missionary was indignant. He interrupted saying, "What I delivered to you were sacred truths, but this that you tell me is mere fable and falsehood." The storyteller told the missionary that he had violated the rules of civility. "My brother, you saw that we, who practiced these rules, believed your stories; why then, do you refuse to credit ours?"[7]

For these Native Americans, courtesy was more important (perhaps more true) than the absolute truth of a story. This attitude was possible because they thought the truth was contextual. That is to say, they made no universal claims for their particular stories, yet, they thought each story was true in the contexts in which they were uttered. "At no point ... does any tribal religion insist that its particular version ... is an absolute historical recording. . . . At best the tribal stories recount how people experienced the creative process which continues today."[8] Native American tribes were capable of understanding that truth is contextual because they lived outside the dominator system. Since no tribe claimed universal validity for its stories, they could value diversity to a far greater extent than people within the dominator system. *These tribes certainly had their wars, but they did not encounter an enemy bent on their total annihilation until their encounter with Europeans.* Mesmerized by the dominator system, these Europeans could not envision an alternative to their morality, intellect and religion. Accordingly, they thought themselves justified in their attempts to destroy or convert (assimilate) the indigenous population.

Native American thinking is still pretty strange to those in the grip of the dominator system; however, it is a way of thinking that is thoroughly consistent with partnership ways. Partnership ways do not understand diversity as an opportunity to rank one different entity over another. They understand that life is strengthened by its diversity. It is, in fact, diversity and not uniformity that enhances life. The problem is not that the way of life in the dominator system is morally bad. The problem is that the dominator system's emphasis on uniformity in thought and deed denies the fact of life's diversity. This will not work for long. The earth cannot accommodate everyone living the same way any more than an ecosystem can accommodate an overabundance of one animal species.[9] Just as diversity of species is essential to the life of the ecosystem, diversity of life style is as crucial to human survival. Abandoning the dominator system's absolutism in thought and action is an essential component of survival.

The Bible challenges the uniform thought of the dominator system with poem, parable and song. We have seen how the Old Testament prophets wrote poetry that challenged the dominator systems in Israel, Judah and Babylon. Their words enabled people to think and envision alternatives to the dominant order. The prophets' poetry stirred up the imagination, and such imagination eventually changed reality. When a person heard the prophet's words, he or she would begin to think in new ways. Accordingly, the prophets created new intellectual paradigms using poetry.[10]

Jesus' parables also attacked the dominator system's one dimensional thinking. We have noted that parables are ambiguous. They can have many faithful interpretations. Accordingly, the meaning of a parable is not clear to those who hear it. One can imagine the reaction of the crowd upon hearing Jesus' parable of the Unjust Steward. He began this parable saying that the rule of God is like a manager who is caught embezzling funds from his employer. *The employer gives him two weeks notice before firing him.* During that time, the manager goes to his employer's creditors and reduces their debt to his employer. If someone owed his boss 100 barrels of wine, the bill would be reduced to 50. If someone else owed 200 bushels of wheat, together they would write 80. When the employer discovered what the manager had done, *he praised the unjust steward for doing such a shrewd thing* (Lk. 16: 1-8). Now I am sure that no one has ever been able to determine one definitive meaning to this parable; however, there is certainly enough in the parable to keep the discussion going for 2000 years.

Indeed, the very fact that this parable does not have one definitive answer reveals its power. Upon hearing such a parable one person would turn to another and ask, "What does that mean?" If the meaning of the parable had been clear, this would not have happened. Because the meaning is ambiguous, a community was created to discuss the parable. In other words, Jesus' ambiguous words created a community in which people will use their imaginations to interpret these ambiguous words. Could it be that the point of the parable is the community it gathers rather than some absolute truth that it was meant to convey? If the actual content of the parable is of less importance than the community that discusses it, then truth resides in the context of the community rather than in some proposition about the parable that seeks to transmit its one and only true meaning.

The language of the dominator system tries to be crystal clear. The dominator system wants to leave nothing to the imagination because when nothing is left for the imagination to imagine, an individual cannot imagine alternative thoughts. Poetry and parables challenge such a state of affairs. They deny absolutes. They recognize that truth can be expressed in a variety of ways and that truth depends more on context than on persistence through time.

Affirming that truth is contextual is the intellectual com-ponent of one's resistance to the dominator system. As long as we maintain the dominator system's contention that truths are absolute, intolerance of others will dominate. Human life may have been able to survive such intolerance in the past, but this capacity for survival decreases with our increasing ability to kill. The dominator system's solution is to have one dominant power such as the United States ruling the world; however, this state of affairs may not be consistent with the long-term survival of humanity. Partnership ways maintain that diversity in thought is in fact supportive of life and survival. Recognizing the fact that truth is contextual is the first step in the appreciating such diversity in thought.

Spiritual Resistance

There are two types of religion. There are religions that serve the dominator system and there are religions influenced by partnership ways. Religions that serve the dominator system provide the rationale for morality to draw the line separating the good from the bad. When this rationale is provided by means of logic, we are engaged in the dominator system's version of theology. When this rationale is provided through worship and ritual, we are engaged in the pageantry that has always been used to support the dominator system.

The Christian religion usually serves the dominator system. It assists the dominator system in the ranking process whenever it makes distinctions between the saved and the damned. When Christians develop intellectual and religious criteria to determine God's elect, they also identify people who are not to be part of God's elect. In the past, this fate has befallen the Jews, immoral people, unbelievers who deny Jesus, people who think they are believers but are not "true" believers, heretics, murderers, thieves, feminists, Lutherans, Roman Catholics, Muslims, Hindus, and other infidels. The list can easily be extended. The point of the list is to illustrate how such distinctions aid the dominator system in its essential ranking process.

The tragic flaw of Christianity is this. *Christianity has always been used by the dominator system; yet, Jesus' entire ministry was in opposition to the dominator system.* It is very difficult to reconcile Jesus to Christianity when Christianity serves the very system that executed Jesus. The same tension between a religion in accord with the dominator system and a religion in accord with partnership ways is present throughout the Old Testament. The Exodus was the first direct conflict between the Biblical God and the dominator system. The 12 tribes that escaped Egyptian captivity immediately attempted to create a system of government that was different from other nations. For over 200 years, they were relatively successful in their attempt to be unlike other nations, but the institution of the monarchy changed this.

The dominator system would have destroyed the Mosaic attempt to form an alternative spirituality were it not for Israel's prophets. They understood religion quite differently from the monarchy. Whereas the monarchy used Temple rituals to support the power structure, the prophets understood the function of religion in a much different way. For example, the prophet Hosea told Israel that God desired mercy and love, not sacrifice (Hos. 6: 6). Amos told this same generation of Israelites that God does not want their sacrifices. God wants them to act justly (Am. 5: 21-24). Jeremiah challenged the ideology of the Judean monarchy, which maintained that Judah could withstand any enemy because it had the Temple of the Lord (Jer. 7: 1-15). Almost every prophet of Israel challenged the monarchy's use of religion. The mere fact that God is supreme meant that God could not be used by Israel's monarchy or any other Empire. Indeed, the prophet Ezekiel was so opposed to religion that used God that he maintained that God is not useful at all.[11]

Since the Bible supports religions that serve partnership ways and opposes religions that are used by the dominator system, it is important to note the characteristics of these two sorts of religion. These characteristics are best illustrated in the stories of Jesus cleansing the Temple (Mt. 21: 12-13; Mk. 11: 15-17; Lk. 19: 45-46, and Jn. 2: 13-22). In cleansing the Temple, Jesus was not opposing capitalism or free enterprise. He was opposing the sacrificial worship practices of the Temple cult because he thought the cult made the Temple "a hideout for robbers" (Mk. 11: 17). When Jesus used this quotation from the prophet Jeremiah, he was saying that the Temple's sacrificial worship practices protected the religious ones from God like a good hideout protects robbers from the police. By making their required sacrifices, religious people believed that they had fulfilled their obligations to God and were counted right with God. Guaranteed of such righteousness, they could do what they pleased without worrying about divine retribution. The sacrifice accorded its practitioners safety. It placated the deity.

Sacrificial religion is not limited to the sacrifice of animals. Sacrificial religion is any religious practice designed to placate the deity. The practice can be ritualistic. It can be moral, or it can just be a matter of correct belief. The key element of sacrificial worship is its *quid pro quo* structure. This structure is very simple. A religious person does something, and God gives something in return. All religions of the dominator system have this *quid pro quo* structure. They do not agree on what the religious person is to do. They do not even agree on what God will give in return, but the religions of the dominator system believe that the deity can be controlled if one sacrifice or another is performed. The religions that serve the dominator system are diverse because almost anything from the sacrifice of virgins to having a strangely warmed heart can be the required element needed to produce divine favor. Such diversity, however, leads to intolerance rather than tolerance because each religion that serves the dominator system has no choice but to say that those who do not perform its own particular act of sacrifice live outside divine favor.

This religious structure leads to a phenomenon peculiar to all religions that serve the dominator system. All demand that the religious people justify themselves. Under the dominator system, religious people have to demonstrate their worthiness to merit God's favor. When an individual argues that he or she is worthy of divine favor, that person is engaged in the act of self-justification. Self-justification has both a moral and religious dimension. One justifies oneself morally though moral argument using the moral criteria established by the culture. One need not use moral argument to justify oneself religiously. All that is necessary is to be declared just by a religious authority. This declaration may be no more troublesome than having one's picture taken with some religious leader, or it may involve a far more difficult demonstration of one's contrite heart. In any case, both religious and moral justifications serve the dominator system because they maintain the line separating the good from the bad and the saints from the sinners.

The need for justification is a consequence of the fact that there is no grace or love in the dominator system. Rules and rituals are always more important than people. The dominator system does not believe that a human being has a basic right to food, clothing, sanitation or shelter. These human needs are never granted simply because a person is in need. These basic needs must be earned by meeting the moral or religious criteria of the established order. A spirituality that supports life is, therefore, impossible within the dominator system. The dominator system's spirituality centers on efforts to justify the self and others. As the prophets note, such self-justification often comes at the expense of those in need.

A spirituality that supports life is quite different. This spirituality has an economic expression in the sense that it gives simply because there is a need. It has a political expression because it recognizes the rights of those in need and presses for and receives remedies to their plight. Spiritualities of life use the power that supports partnership ways.

One of the most important features of the movement from religions of the dominator system to religions of partnership is the rejection of self-justification. Refusing to justify oneself can have dangerous consequences. Jesus' presence before Pilate is a profound example of both Jesus' refusal to justify himself and the

149

penalty he paid for such a refusal. Jesus was silent before Pilate. He did not answer his questions. This left Pilate with "no alternative" but crucifixion.

It is one thing to say that a person should refuse to justify herself. It is quite another to address how one is to do this. The first step in this dangerous and difficult enterprise is to recognize what self-justification is and what it is not. A personal example from my work as a pastor might help. As most people know, the Church distinguishes between laity and clergy. In most denominations, clergy have certain functions that lay people are "forbidden" to do except under "extraordinary" circumstances. I happen to be against these distinctions. I believe that there is nothing that a pastor can do that a layperson cannot do. I often express this belief publicly.

In my Lutheran domination, laypersons are routinely excluded from presiding at Holy Communion. They can preach. They can establish congregational policy. They can teach. They can do anything but preside at Holy Communion. Evidently, Holy Communion is just a little too holy for them. As noted, I am against this practice. I am against it because it promotes a distinction between clergy and laity that ranks clergy above laity in the divine order of things. Accordingly, it perpetuates the dominator system.

I also tell the congregation that, in the absence of another ordained pastor, I will be the only one in the congregation who will preside at Holy Communion. The usual justification Lutheran pastors give for this position is that the clerical monopoly on the celebration of sacraments promotes "good order." As near as I can tell, "good order" is a phrase used whenever pastors routinely do things they have no good reason to do. "Good order" is used in this case because there is no good reason to prohibit laypeople from presiding at Holy Communion. This practice is even contrary to Martin Luther's contention that a person's baptism makes that person a priest, bishop and pope. Luther went on to coin the phrase "the priesthood of all believers" in an effort to abolish the Church's habit of ranking priests above laity in the divine scheme of things.

Despite these facts, I do not want lay people to preside at Holy Communion in congregations that I serve; however, I do not

larly difficult undertaking because religions under the sway
dominator system have obscured the power of confession.
se religious circles, a sin or misdeed is confessed and then
ed. The person who confesses acknowledges that he or she
he wrong side of the moral divide. The absolution simply
s that person on the proper side of the moral divide. The
ator system's basic moral structure remains intact.

*The purpose of confession is different in religions and
alities that support partnership ways. These religions use
ion to fight evil.* The reason for this has to do with the
of evil itself. *Evil is a seemingly autonomous force in
ion to life. It originates in the refusal or inability to
ledge and confess one's sins, misdeeds or mistakes.* The
ng example illustrates this description. If I tell a
larly unflattering lie about you, a number of things might
. At best, the person to whom I told the lie does not repeat
is case, the damage is minimal. At worst, the lie is repeated
eated and repeated again. Everyone hears it. You begin to
that people are treating you differently, and you cannot
and why. You ask your best friend, but she does not want
ass it. After much provocation, however, she tells you her
of my lie. You, of course, deny the allegation. This does
ate your friend in the least. She assumed you would deny
gation because people like you never tell the truth.

We can gain control of evil by confession. In this exam-
r life in the community is undermined as long as I do not
my lie to the community. Things change if I confess. The
ity regains control of the situation. The community must

The character of evil is exposed in this example. My lie
ed a power that is opposed to your life in the community.
our life in the community contributes to the community's
power that my lie unleashed is also in opposition to the
the community. This power seems to be autonomous. It
to have a life all its own. No one controls it. It goes
r the lie is told, and does whatever damage it does. Evil,
, is not exactly autonomous. In this case its source is my
to acknowledge and confess the lie. Hence, evil is a
ly autonomous force in opposition to life that originates in
sal or inability to acknowledge and confess one's sins,
s or mistakes.

We can gain control of evil by confession. In this exam-
r life in the community is undermined as long as I do not
my lie to the community. Things change if I confess. The
ity regains control of the situation. The community must

give "good order" as a reason. I do not attempt to justify my
inconsistency in any way. I merely state that I do not want to
spend the rest of my life engaged in a controversy with my
bishops, some clergy and some laypeople in my denomination
over this issue. I tell people who have the need to preside –
perhaps the God-given need – to gather some like-minded people
and do it. I ask that they do not do this in my presence. I simply do
not want the hassle.

Note, this is not a self-justification. It is an explanation.
The distinction between the two is important. I owe the people an
explanation, but I need not justify myself when I explain myself.
*An explanation merely states the reasons for an action or a belief.
It does not try to make these reasons into a virtue. A justification
always attempts to make the reasons for a particular belief or
practice into a virtue. A justification always tries to claim the
moral high ground.*

The example above is a good illustration of the difference
between an explanation and a justification because no attempt was
made to claim the high moral ground. Indeed, neither the action
nor the reason for the action has any possible claim to virtue. A
person with more character or more conviction may well have
acted in a more admirable way, but I happen to be too tired to fight
this battle. My explanation is, however, the truth. I cannot justify
my refusal to allow laypersons to preside at Holy Communion. I
can only explain why I do not want this to happen in a
congregation I serve.

This distinction between an explanation and a justification
is a very important component in efforts to move from religions
under the dominator system to spiritualities that affirm partnership
ways. Unfortunately, it is not an easy distinction to understand
because we are under the sway of the dominator system. Under the
dominator system, survival may depend on remaining on the
proper side of the line. Poverty, imprisonment and premature
death await those who cross this moral divide. Self-justification is
a way to defend ourselves from these fates. When something is
amiss, we are taught to justify ourselves or at least find someone
else to blame. Justification and blaming are two survival tools of
the dominator system. No one will admit responsibility even, or
especially, in the higher levels of the dominator system. As I write,
President Bush's National Security Advisor is blaming others for

the failure to predict September 11, and men and women in the previous Democratic administration are trying to absolve themselves as well. This is understandable given our subservience to the dominator system.

This is also the reason why people will always think you are justifying yourself when you are merely explaining yourself. Justification and blame are employed so often that everyone is inclined to confuse them with a mere explanation. It is, therefore, very important to make it clear that an explanation rather than a justification is being offered. This distinction must be made within the conversation itself. It must be repeated often. The one offering the explanation must make it clear that he or she is not seeking the moral high ground but is only giving the reasons for the action or belief. This is different from the one engaged in self-justification. This person is not just narrating his or her reasons. This person is asserting that these reasons are pure, right and good. This person is attempting to demonstrate moral superiority.

Everyday life becomes very different when one remembers and communicates the distinction between an explanation and justification. For example, a husband and wife will argue much differently if they try to justify themselves instead of explain themselves. In their attempts at self-justification, both husband and wife desire to be understood as the virtuous one. If the wife "wins" the argument, then she is also considered the more virtuous. If, as is usually the case, no one "wins," each partner leaves thinking that their mate has a character flaw, and each begins to wonder if this flaw is grounds to terminate the relationship. Efforts to justify oneself undermine the life of our most intimate relationships. A marriage has little to gain and much to loose from such efforts.

If, on the other hand, the goal of an argument is to explain, there will be more give and take. Compromise will be possible, and growth in the relationship will be more likely. This is because the purpose of the argument is to explain oneself without claiming the moral high ground. Furthermore, the reasons your partner offers are not a threat to your virtue. They are ways to find out what is important. Understanding and being understood are the goals of those who seek to explain themselves. Being declared righteous is the goal of those who seek to justify themselves. This is an important thing to know because the declaration of righteousness is usually accomplished at the expense of the other.

There is seldom enough righteousness for hand, there is usually enough understandin

Recognizing the difference betwe planation has practical implications in business that seeks justification is like environment than one where people seek are less likely to be tolerated in e justification because established policies h sort of moral virtue. It takes much m alternatives to policies and proposals th than it does to suggest alternatives to poli effective. Everyone knows that there are effectiveness. Few recognize improveme moral purity. If the conversations merel one will claim the moral high ground. more open and far more creative.

Attempts to justify ourselves are mine individual and social relationsh disastrous consequences within the poli bin Ladan and George Bush believe th ones. Both believe they are justified. As have a moral right to kill innocent peopl use to justify themselves differ because distinguish between good and evil in dif each man believes that justice, goodnes Each man fervently believes that his acti Yet, life itself is depleted because of beliefs of such men and their followers.

The purpose of a religion gover tem is to justify the moral line separati This justification is both rational an spiritual quest is to demonstrate that he side of the moral divide. Self-justificati the tools whereby one's goodness is de serves partnership ways has different co

Partnership religions abandon explanation and confession. We explanation can promote well bei justification. A discussion of confessio

partic
of the
In the
absolv
is on
restore
domin

spiritu
confes
nature
opposi
acknov
follow
particu
happer
it. In th
and rep
notice
underst
to disc
version
not pla
the alle

unleash
Since y
life, the
life of
appears
wherev
howeve
refusal
seeming
the refu
misdeec

ple, you
confess
commur

now decide what to do about me. The consequences might be quite severe for me, but the consequences are under the community's control. Evil is no longer operative.

Confession is the way to regain control of evil. It is the opposite of both self-justification and blaming others. Both justification and blaming locate difficulties on the outside. If I justify myself, then someone else is the source of the calamity. If I blame someone else, then the blamed one is responsible and not me. Confession, on the other hand, tries to understand one's own contribution to the difficulties. Confession is not the guilt-seeking enterprise that it has become under the influence of the dominator system. It is not designed to paralyze someone with guilt. Confession is the most important tool in the fight against evil. An honest confession controls evil and prevents it from opposing life. A truthful confession is not easy. We risk losing our stature when we confess. Nonetheless, confession is a fundamental component in the fight against evil.

It is one thing when individuals refuse to acknowledge and confess sins or misdeeds. The consequences are far more severe when groups, communities or nations refuse to acknowledge and confess their sins. Recently the pedophilia of a number of Roman Catholic priests has become public. What is even more damaging than the individual priestly crimes, however, is the fact that these crimes were known but not confessed for so many years. Bishops knew of the crimes. Their response was a cover-up. They paid off or silenced the victims, and they merely relocated the culprits to other parishes. Many of these priestly culprits continued their crimes against humanity at their new congregations. In its refusal to acknowledge and confess its crime, the Church hierarchy unleashed the power of evil. There is no telling the damage that this has done to the Church in general, to the world and most especially to the victims of these tragic crimes. The damage was, however, a direct result of evil – the seemingly autonomous force against life that exists because we refuse to acknowledge and confess our sins. A quick and timely confession of these sins to the community and the world would have prevented so much destruction. It is particularly tragic because it happened within a community that should have known that confession resists evil. The Roman Catholic Church did not remember this because, like most of Christianity, it serves the dominator system. Accordingly, it had relegated confession and absolution to merely reestablishing the absolved one to his or her place on the proper side of morality's divide.

The power of evil is often a force in international affairs. This too is a consequence of the refusal or inability to acknowledge and confess wrongdoings. Our current struggle against terrorists is a prime example. The United States believes that the attacks against it were unprovoked. The President wonders why people hate us, and most U.S. citizens firmly believe that there was no reason for the attacks. This being the case, we are quick to say that the terrorists who attacked us and killed so many Americans on September 11, 2001 are the sole source of evil in this affair. Accordingly, the United States thinks it is justified to use whatever force is necessary in order to destroy the evil of terrorism.

Once again, we believe that the enemy is the only source of evil. This belief prevents us from exploring all of the possible reasons for attacks against our citizens. Note, what follows is not a justification for the attacks. There is no justification for the attacks. The people who planned and carried out the attacks are murderers; however, the fact that the United States was a victim of murderous thugs does not mean that we cannot be a little introspective and look for an answer to the question the President asked, namely, "Why do they hate us?" If we ask this question, we might find some reasons. We will never find a justification. We might simply find some reasons, and, in finding these reasons, we may be able to avoid some similar occurrences in the future.

Many nations in the world see the United States of America as a source of terror. They use recent political events as evidence. In the 1980s, the United States conducted a war against the duly elected government of Nicaragua. We armed insurgents who we called "contras," and we blockaded and mined Nicaragua's harbors. (One can only imagine what would have happened to a nation so foolish as to blockade and mine our harbors.) Nicaragua did not retaliate. Nicaragua took us to court. Our actions were condemned by the World Court for terrorist activities. We are at present the only nation in the world to be so condemned. The General Assembly of the United Nations with only Israel and San Salvador casting negative votes also condemned our actions against Nicaragua. The only reason these actions were not condemned in the Security Council of the United Nations is that the United States vetoed the proposal.[13]

In 1998, the Clinton administration attacked an al-Shira pharmaceutical plant in the Sudan. The administration believed that the plant was producing weapons of mass destruction. These allegations were probably false, but even if they are true, the United States itself produces such weapons. In any case, this attack led to tens of thousands of deaths in the Sudan because the attack destroyed the Sudanese pharmaceutical industry. These estimates of casualties were made by three separate sources: Human Rights Watch; Werner Daum, the German Ambassador to the Sudan in a review in *Harvard International Review* (Summer 2001); and Jonathan Belke, the Regional Director of Near East Foundation, in the August, 22 1999 edition of *The Boston Globe*.[14] These events, combined with our near 50 year blockade of Cuba, bombing of Lybia, invasions of Granada and Panama, our support of Israel not to mention our conflicts in Iraq and Viet Nam might give an answer to the President's question, "Why do they hate us?" Perhaps those who do not like us are uninformed or merely do not understand the "obvious" distinction between destruction at the hands of friendly Americans and the hostile actions of terrorists. The fact of the matter is, however, that the only way through the current international crisis is for everyone to acknowledge the possibility of their wrongdoing. Confession, instead of self-justification and/or blaming the enemy for all the evil in the world, may be a path to a more peaceful world.

Explanation and confession are spiritual tools people who resist the dominator system can employ. When we explain ourselves rather than justify ourselves, we are more likely to breathe life into our relationships. Compromise and understanding are more likely to occur and enrich our relationships. Self-justification tends to undermine our relationships because we try to claim the moral high ground when we justify ourselves. In the end, this hurts our relationships because such a practice insists on a winner and a loser. In insisting on a winner and a loser, justification also insists on ranking the winner above the loser; hence, the equality of the relationship is destroyed.

Confession is also a spiritual tool that resists the dominator system. Confession limits the power of evil. Evil does not reside in the other as dominator religions maintain. Evil is the autonomous force against life that comes into existence when we do not acknowledge and confess our sins and misdeeds. Confession refuses to locate all evil in the enemy. Instead, confession helps us see some of ourselves in the enemy. It enables us to learn from our enemy. So understood, the enemy still might be the enemy, but the humanity of the enemy is not denied. As such, our relationship to the enemy is transformed. In the end, therefore, how one understands one's enemies is the principle issue of partnership religions and spiritualities. Do we only find evil in our enemies as the religions of the dominator system assert, or can we also see ourselves in our enemies.[15]

Communal Resistance

Less than 10,000 demonstrators remained in Tiananmen Square. They were surrounded by the Chinese army. As they waited for the inevitable, it was discovered that some demonstrators were armed. Chai Ling called the group together. She told the demonstrators a story about a huge colony of over a billion ants that lived on a high mountain. A fire was set at the base of the mountain and threatened to consume the colony of ants. The ants decided to make themselves into a gigantic ball, and they rolled down the mountain to safety. The ants on the surface of the ball died, but the ants protected by those on the surface lived.

Chai Ling told the demonstrators that they were the ones on the surface. They must die for the people of China. The demonstrators destroyed their weapons and waited for certain attack.[16] Because they did not meet violence with violence, the Chinese demonstrators exposed the Chinese version of the dominator system for what it is. It is a system based upon the power of death. It is a system that can be resisted by people willing to die for life.

Commenting on his own impending death at the hands of the dominator system, Jesus said, "I am telling you the truth. A grain of wheat is useless unless it falls to the earth and dies. But if it falls to the earth and dies, it bears much fruit (Jn. 12: 24).

The dominator system would have us believe that resistance is futile. It would say that the crucifixion of Jesus brought an end to Jesus' power. It would say that the force used in the Tiananmen Square massacre only demonstrates the power of the

Chinese dominator system to destroy its opposition. These beliefs are not exactly true. Jesus' crucifixion continued the movement Jesus had begun, and, for a while, it made this movement much stronger than it was during Jesus' lifetime. The Tiananmen Square massacre may have been no more an end to the Chinese resistance than the Amritsar massacre ended the Indian struggle against the British version of the dominator system. People may not think the Amritsar massacre is the best parallel to the Tiananmen Square massacre, but this is only because our memories are so short. The Amritsar massacre happened in 1919. In their effort to maintain their domination of India, the British slaughtered thousands of unarmed Punjabis. It is said that the British fired until they ran out of ammunition. This massacre did not silence the Indian people. It may have increased their resolve. The British left India less than thirty years later. They did not leave because they graciously abandoned their dominance. They left because they could no longer govern India. The same could happen to China's version of the dominator system. It too could cease to exist.[17]

Resistance to the dominator system is not as futile as most people think. In the past 60 years, we have witnessed victories over the dominator system in India's struggle for independence from Britain and in the African American struggle against segregation in the United States. We have seen the Soviet Union collapse and many other nations remove dictators without firing a shot. The dominator system can be successfully resisted. Sometimes it can even be stopped, but this requires people who are willing to face death. Resistance is possible, but it requires courage. It requires the conviction that life is worth the risk of death.

The courage to risk death permeates the being of a person who resists the dominator system. This courage is exhibited in the life of Jesus. It is possessed by Jesus' disciples. In recent years, this courage has been exhibited by women like Chai Ling, men like Mohatma Gandhi, couples like Nelson and Winnie Mandela and movements like the American civil rights movement and Poland's Solidarity. Those who resist have discovered that the dominator system only has the power to kill. When this is accepted, then the power of life that is present in partnership ways can overcome the dominator system.

159

From time to time, the dominator system does its work very well. It uses violence and silences the opposition. This fact must not be underestimated. Violence can work. Simone Weil rejected Marxism because her experience taught her that the hoped for victory of the proletariat was not guaranteed. Marx taught that the weight of the suffering of the proletariat would become so great that they would inevitably rise up and throw off their chains, but Weil came to believe that such suffering did not guarantee revolution. The violence of the dominator system can be so oppressive and the suffering so severe that people are not capable of speech much less revolution. People suffer in silence when oppression becomes most severe.[18]

Mute suffering is the sort of suffering that the dominator system seeks to promote. It is in the interest of the dominator system because when suffering is silent, the decent people of the world can pretend that no one suffers. When suffering is exposed, those who suffer sometimes receive very powerful advocates, and the absolute power of the dominator system is undermined. This is probably what happened in the civil rights movement in the 1950s and 1960s. African Americans had been suffering under the weight of racism since coming to America. Much of this suffering was in silence until the media exposed the violence of America's version of apartheid for the world to see. Exposed to the light of day, attempts were made to abolish this form of oppression.

The success or failure of resistance to the dominator system seems to depend on the existence of supportive and informed communities. The Biblical witness demonstrates the need for such communities. It was not enough for the Hebrew slaves to merely escape Egyptian domination. They formed a community that was designed to be an alternative to the dominator system. Moses' father-in-law, Jethro, established a decentralized system of judges to rule Israel. He did this because he recognized that Israel could not be organized like other nations and still be an alternative to the dominator system.

Likewise, the communities that met in the name of Jesus were also designed to be an alternative to the dominant culture. Since there are many ways to be an alternative community, early Christians ordered themselves in different ways. We have seen that Luke spoke of a community where all property was held in common and each received according to each person's need (Acts

4: 32-35). Matthew's community seems to have been a listening community (Mt. 18: 15-18). In such a community, people influenced each other. They took each other seriously and made adjustments in their lives on the basis of what they had heard. In this respect, they were imitating Jesus who also made adjustments in his life on the basis of human need. Adjustments are indeed made in the dominator system, but it is always the less powerful or lower rank that adjusts to the more powerful. In Mathew's listening community, those of higher rank also made adjustments to those of lower rank. Such a practice is neither normal nor desirable within the dominator system. Finally, Paul's vision of an alternative community was one in which ranking does not occur. He believed that there ought to be no distinction between male and female, Jew and Gentile or slave and free in a community that was formed in the spirit of Jesus (Gal. 3: 26).

Alternative communities support our resistance to the dominator system in three important ways. First, they create a safe haven for the intellectual task of discerning the character of resistance. As we have seen, such resistance has ethical, intellectual, religious and political dimensions, and intellectual reflection is often necessary in order to discern how best to resist.

Second, alternative communities allow people to practice resistance in every day life. For the most part, resistance to the dominator system happens in the small areas of life. It happens in families, classrooms, businesses and among friends. It usually involves a simple act here or a simple statement there. Although the activity is normally small and mundane, carrying out an act of resistance usually involves courage on the part of the actor because each small act of resistance can result in a loss. A person might lose a friend. Conflict might arise between loved ones. Even jobs can be lost. An alternative community acts as a safety net in these instances. It helps support those who have lost something due to their resistance. One can imagine, for example, how someone who resisted the dominator system at work would have benefited from being a member of an alternative community like the one Luke described in Acts. If a person lives in a community where all material goods are held in common and each receives in accord with his or her needs, then that person can more readily risk losing a job. The risks inherent in resistance would be eased considerably by participation in such a community.

Although resistance is practiced in small areas of life, these small confrontations sometimes snowball into large-scale confrontations with the dominator system. Rosa Parks performed a small act of resistance the day that she was arrested for refusing to give up her seat on that Montgomery, Alabama bus, but Rosa Parks was not alone that day. She was an officer in the NAACP. The communities to which she belonged trained her in non-violent resistance. She was ready for a confrontation. Her resistance could not have started the civil rights movement, however, if the people were not ready to act. Jo Ann Gibson, the President of the Woman's Political Council, had already threatened the Montgomery city officials with a boycott if the conditions on the buses were not improved. Her council had plans to distribute fifty thousand notices of a boycott. When she heard of Park's arrest, she set her distribution system in motion. Practically every man, woman and child in Montgomery knew about the bus boycott within a few hours.[19] At the beginning of the civil rights movement, alternative communities like the NAACP, the Woman's Political Council and the African American churches of Montgomery transformed Rosa Park's small courageous act – an act that simply could have meant jail time for Rosa Parks – into a national movement of resistance to the apartheid-like practices of the American dominator system. This is the third way alternative communities can support resistance to the dominator system. These communities prevent the small mundane acts of resistance like the arrest of Rosa Parks from lapsing into silence. These communities also provided the support for the larger struggle that may come. Without such support, individual resistance often comes to nothing.

Although alternative communities assume a variety of forms, they do hold one important characteristic in common. *Alternative communities refuse to employ the sort of power that the dominator system uses.* The dominator system uses unilateral power. As has been noted, unilateral power operates from a power center. It seeks to move the external world without being moved by the external world.[20] Unilateral power is very effective because the threat of death backs it up. Sometimes the threat of death is clearly articulated. Other times it is understated. It is always understood. The Pharaoh used unilateral power in his attempt to control the Hebrew slaves. Unilateral power was used by the religious and political leaders of Rome to execute Jesus. Unilateral power is at the center of American foreign policy. Civilizations and people of the dominator system always employ unilateral power. They see no alternative. They believe that unilateral power is the only kind of power there is.

Communities that resist the dominator system refrain from using unilateral power. They often use communal power instead. Like unilateral power, communal power tries to influence the external world. Unlike unilateral power, those who employ communal power also expect to be influenced by the external world.[21] Centers of communal power are willing to change if such change will enhance the life of the world. In other words, communal power makes adjustments on the basis of what is communicated by the external world. Listening must, therefore, be an important skill in the use of communal power because listening also involves making an adjustment based upon what the other parties in the conversation have communicated. Such adjustments are not only based on what other human beings are saying. Other living species communicate as well, and adjustments should be made on the basis of what these living things are communicating. Life on the planet earth may depend on the existence of alternative communities who listen to non-human life. We are only beginning to understand the importance of this skill. Such skills, however, are indicative of the partnership notion that life is a diverse web. Since each portion of the web enriches the whole, life can only benefit if adjustments are made based upon communication from other forms of life.

The Bible narrates many conflicts between the dominator system and partnership ways. The Exodus was a victory of a partnership way over the dominator system. The rise and triumph of Israel's monarchy was a victory of the dominator system over partnership ways. Jesus championed a partnership way. The Church generally preferred the dominator system. The Bible itself sometimes supports the dominator system at the expense of partnership ways. The patriarchal treatment of women in the Old Testament, and to a lesser extent in the New Testament, is tragic commentary on Biblical writers' inability to escape the dominion of the dominator system. Nonetheless, the Bible does tell the story of a struggle between the dominator system and partnership ways. We have forgotten about this struggle because we are so engrained in the dominator system that we cannot see alternatives even when these alternatives occur right in front of our eyes. Our amnesia is intentional, but it is intended by the dominator system itself.

The Bible discloses a variety of ways the dominator system can be resisted. We have discussed intellectual, religious, moral, political and social ways in this book. We must end with the reminder that the Bible does not exhaust the subject of resistance. Resistance has occurred in many different ways, in many places and in a variety of different contexts. The people of Israel, Jesus and his followers were once engaged in this now forgotten struggle. It is important for people committed to this Biblical God to remember this forgotten struggle and to continue it in new ways.

End Notes

Introduction: The Extent of Our Amnesia

[1] Daniel Quinn, *Providence: the Story of a Fifty-Year Vision Quest* (New York: Bantam Books, 1994) p. 150.

[2] George M. Frederickson, "Slaves and Race: the Southern Dilemma," *American Negro Slavery: A Modern Reader*, edited by Allen Weinstein, Frank Otto Gatell and David Sarrsohn (New York: Oxford University Press, 1979) p.38.

[3] Walter Brueggemann, *The Prophetic Imagination* (Philadelphia: Fortress Press, 1978) p. 30.

[4] Ibid, pp. 28-43.

[5] It is difficult to understand how the belief that Biblical inspiration depends on the Bible being unerring in every detail. The Bible contradicts itself in some places. It begins with two creation stories in Genesis 1 and Genesis 2. These stories have different orders to creation. Genesis 1 says that humanity was created both male and female on the afternoon of the sixth day. Genesis 2 says that Adam was formed from the earth before there was any vegetation or animal life. Then vegetation and animal life were created and then the woman, Eve, was created out of Adam's rib. To cite another example, Matthew, Mark and Luke all say that Jesus cleansed the Temple on the Sunday before his crucifixion. In contrast, John has Jesus cleansing the Temple at the beginning of his three year ministry. There are many more examples of inconsistencies within the Biblical narrative itself. One or the other account has to be inaccurate unless we agree to suspend our normal ways of understanding reality when we read the Bible.

Chapter 1: The Bible's Forgotten Context

[1] Jay G. Williams, "Expository Article: Genesis 3," *Interpretation: A Journal of Biblical Theology,* Vol. 35, No. 3, July, 1981, p. 278.

[2] When Jesus and his disciples encounter a blind man in the 9th chapter of John, they reflect this view of infirmity when they ask, "Master, who sinned, the man or his parents, that he was born blind." The Book of Job also examines this theological position in much more detail.

[3] Raine Eisler, *The Chalice and the Blade: Our History, Our Future* (San Francisco: Harper, 1988). In this deeply profound work, Eisler offers us a

paradigm shift for the way we view most everything. In this book, I am using Eisler's paradigm shift to understand and to interpret the Bible.
[4] Ibid., p.57.
[5] Ibid., p. xvii.
[6] Ibid., pp.1-41. In a very real way, my use of the word "discovery" is no more appropriate than the use of the word in the phrase, "Columbus discovered America." Just as there were already people living in the Western Hemisphere when Columbus "discovered" it, Native Americans and other people in the world still live in accord with partnership ways. These ways may be in danger of extinction, but those who still remember or live in accord with partnership ways would be surprised to find they have just been "discovered." I ask forgiveness when I use the word discover. I use the word here to distinguish partnership ways from a utopian mental construct. Partnership ways exist, have existed, and our future may depend on them flourishing in the near future.
[7] Ibid., p. xvii, xix, 7-41, 198-203.
[8] Vine Deloria, Jr. *God is Red: A Native View of Religion Thirtieth Anniversary Edition* (Golden Colorado: Fulcrum Publishing) p. 88.
[9] Ibid., p. 87.
[10] Eisler, pp. 43, 44. Italics mine.
[11] Daniel Quinn's theories are developed in the following philosophical novels: *Ishmael* (New York: Bantam/Turner Books, 1992). *The Story of B* (New York: Bantam Books, 1996). *My Ishmael* (New York: Bantam Books, 1997). He also has written an autobiography, *Providence: The Story of a Fifty-Year Vision Quest* (New York: Bantam Books, 1994), and a non-fiction work called *Beyond Civilization: Humanity's Next Great Adventure* (New York: Three Rivers Press, 1999).
[12] One must keep in mind that a technology is more an efficient way of doing something than it is a machine. Machines may well be a sub set of technology, but technology includes much more than machines. See Preface pp. ii, iii.
[13] Quinn, *My Ishmael*, p. 61.
[14] Ibid. The phrase food placed "under lock and key" will be used frequently throughout this book. Whenever it is used, the words "under lock and key" will be in quotes. I hope that these quotation marks will remind the reader of the great debt owed to Quinn in this analysis of the Bible.
[15] For a wonderful account of the relationship between medical technology to medical practice, writing to the human brain, television to attention span and community read Neil Postman, *Technopoly: The Surrender of Culture to Technology* (New York: Alfred A. Knopf, 1992).
[16] This was not the only social/political innovation caused by the printing press. Neil Postmann, *The Disappearance of Childhood (New York: Vintage Books, 1994)* notes that the printing press created childhood

itself. Prior to the printing press, the Church said that the age of reason was achieved at age 7. This age was chosen because in medieval society a person would have learned just about all he or she needed to know by that age. All that was needed was the physical powers necessary to do the tasks assigned by an individual's station in life. After the invention of the printing press, however, more time was needed for someone to learn what their culture needed them to learn. Specifically, young people needed to learn how to read. There came to be a distinction between adults and children. Indeed, one is hard pressed to state the qualities of adulthood that are not also qualities necessary to read a book. To name but a few qualities adults and readers share, one has to be able to sit still, defer gratification and possess some tolerance for boredom.

[17] Quinn, *Ishmael*, pp. 151-184.

[18] Deloria, pp. 61-76.

[19] Quinn, *Ishmael*, pp. 108, 109.

[20] Norman F. Cantor, *The Civilization of the Middle Ages* (New York: Harper Perennial, 1994) p. 5. It might even be argued on the basis of this book that one of the accomplishments of medieval Christianity was to preserve the dominator system within a more or less "Christian" framework. Medieval Christians were in fact very successful in this endeavor. The endeavor, however, cannot be said to have been faithful to Jesus.

[21] This is not just ancient history. The option to assimilate or die was presented to most of the Native population in the continental United States during the 19th century. The Native population of South Africa also received the same option during and after their colonial periods.

[22] Quinn, *Beyond Civilization*, p. 37.

[23] Jeremy Sabloft, "Maya," *Encyclopedia Americana – International Edition* (Danbury, Conn.: Grolier, 1992) as discussed in Quinn *Beyond Civilization*, p. 41.

[24] Quinn, *Beyond Civilization*, p. 38.

[25] Ibid., p. 39.

[26] Ibid., p. 41.

Chapter 2: Israel's Exodus

1 Alice Laffey, *An Introduction to the Old Testament: A Feminist Perspective* (Philadelphia: Fortress Press, 1988) p. 47.

[2] Ibid., pp. 46-48.

[3] Ibid., p. 52.

[4] God's anger with Moses did not end here. Apparently, the God of Israel had second thoughts about the selection of Moses and tried to kill him. Moses' wife, Zipporah saved him by circumcising their son. (Ex. 4: 24-

26). This strange story makes a little more sense if we remember all of the objections Moses made to his mission. Moses' separation from Israel was revealed both in these objections and by the fact that Moses had not had his son circumcised. It is no wonder that God had second thoughts on the matter of Moses' selection. Finally, it is only the faithful actions of Zipporah that both saved Moses' life and reestablished Moses' family's relationship to Israel. Zipporah was yet another woman who saved Moses' life. See Laffey, pp. 48-51.

[5] Eisler, pp. 54-56.

[6] Deloria, pp. 97-112.

[7] Contemporary examples of this phenomenon abound. Toward the end of the reign of South African apartheid, Winnie Mandela's body guards were accused and perhaps convicted of some violent crime. She received a good deal of bad press because of this. No one, however, ever asked the question, "Why does Winnie Mandela need body guards in the first place?" Could it be that the "order' under which she lived was violent? In a similar vein, Gandhi exposed the violence of British colonialism. Martin Luther King Jr. exposed the violence of the segregated South. The Chinese students exposed the violence of the regime in China. Nonviolence appears to be the best tool in exposing the dominator system's reliance on violence.

[8] The name that God gave Moses can be translated, "I am who I am" or "I am who I will be." This name stands in stark contrast to the claim of the dominator system which says that *its* view of reality is the only understanding that *is* possible or *will be* possible.

[9] Terence E. Fretheim, *Exodus: Interpretation A Biblical Commentary for Teaching and Preaching* (Louisville: John Knox Press, 1991) p. 115.

[10] Ibid., p.116.

[11] Walter Brueggemann, *The Prophetic Imagination* (Philadelphia: Fortress Press, 1972) p. 20.

[12] Fretheim, pp. 121,122.

[13] It is interesting to note that every time Moses makes a request to the Pharaoh, Moses asks that the people be allowed to go into the desert for three days or so in order to worship their God. The issue, at least as it is presented to the Pharaoh, actually is the toleration of a different religion or way of life *within* the Egyptian dominator system. The dominator system, however, cannot allow an alternative.

[14] Fretheim, p. 130.

Chapter 3: Building an Alternative Community

[1] Walter Brueggemann may have coined the phrase "alternative community" in his book *The Prophetic Imagination,* pp. 11-27. It is at

least the first place that I heard of this helpful description of the Mosaic agenda. We would do well to use and develop the practical dimensions of this idea in any effort to seek alternatives to the dominator system.

[2] Claus Westermann, *Creation* translated by John J. Scullion, S.J.(Philadelphia: Fortress Press, 1974) p. 61.

[3] Ibid., pp. 82,83.

[4] Exodus 20. There are other, slightly different versions of the Commandments in the Bible. See Deuteronomy 5 for example.

[5] The greatest appropriation of stolen land happened with the Treaty of Tordesillas in 1494. In keeping with Pope Alexander VI *Inter Caetera Bull* of 1493, the Pope divided the lands of North and South America between the Portuguese and the Spanish. In other words, the Pope gave North and South America away. This action is like me giving your house away, but on a much larger scale. Few Europeans thought that the Pope's action was a violation of the commandment against stealing. Indeed, the Pope's action gave the political arm of the dominator society the moral authority it needed to kill and rape the inhabitants of their newly acquired "properties." This is another example of how the religious and the political unite in the dominator system. See Deloria, pp. 257-270.

[6] Robert W. Jenson, *A Large Catechism* (Delhi, New York: American Lutheran Publicity Bureau, 1991) p.11.

[7] Sharon Ringe, *Jesus, Liberation and the Biblical Jubilee: Images for Ethics and Christology* (Philadelphia: Fortress Press, 1985)

[8] Ibid, p. 19.

[9] The fact that Christians actually think that their God is omnipotent, omniscient and unchanging only indicates how the dominator system has taken over Christianity. It also indicates our Biblical illiteracy, for, on numerous occasions, the God of the Bible does not exhibit these attributes. Such attributes must be redefined if they are to still be employed in reference to the Biblical God.

[10] Brevard Childs, *The Book of Exodus: An Old Testament Library*, (Philadelphia: Westminster Press, 1974) p. 567 ff.

[11] Terrance Fretheim, *The Suffering of God: An Old Testament Perspective* (Philadelphia: Fortress Press, 1984) p.51.

Chapter 4: The Collapse of the Mosaic Alternative

[1] George Mendenhall, "The Monarchy," *Interpretation.* 29 (1975) p. 158. This article was discussed in Walter Brueggemann, *The Prophetic Imagination* (Philadelphia: Fortress Press, 1978) p. 31 ff. As the following notes indicate, my ideas of concerning the collapse of the Mosaic alternative are greatly influence by Brueggemann's work.

[2] Mendenhall, p. 159.

[3] Ibid., p. 164.

[4] Walter Brueggemann, *The Prophetic Imagination* p. 31.

[5] Ibid., p. 37.

[6] Ibid., p. 35.

[7] Ibid., p. 37.

[8] Walter Brueggemann, *Hopeful Imagination: Prophetic Voices in Exile* (Philadelphia: Fortress Press, 1986) p. 52.

[9] Ibid, p. 82.

[10] Ibid., pp. 96-99.

[11] Walter Wink, *Engaging the Powers: Discernment and Resistance in a World of Domination* (Minneapolis: Fortress Press, 1992) p. 12-30. This book won three Book of the Year awards. In my opinion this third part of a trilogy was the theological book of the last decade. I have yet to read a better one both from the perspective of writing style and content.

[12] Walter Wink, *The Powers That Be: Theology for a New Millennium* (New York: Doubleday, 1998) p. 48-62.

[13] See Wink, *Engaging the Powers,* pp. 17-31 or *The Powers that Be* pp. 48-62 for the best, most creative and comprehensive analysis of our culture's attachment to the myth of redemptive violence. I do not do justice to his creative work. What follows is an attempt to summarize Winks views. I happen to agree with them in all respects, but they originate with him. He even appears to have coined the phrase "myth of redemptive violence."

[14] Ibid, pp.18.

[15] Ibid.

[16] Ibid.

[17] Ibid., pp. 19, 20.

[18] Ibid., pp. 25-31.

[19] Paul Kennedy, *The Rise and Fall of the Great Powers: Economic Change and Military Conflict from 1500 to* 2000 (New York: Random House, 1987).

[20] See Jacques Ellul, *The Humiliation of the Word* translated by Joyce Main Hanks (Grand Rapids, Michigan: Wm. Eerdmanns, 1985) pp. 5-111 for a far more profound argument for the fact that modern culture has depreciated the value of words in favor of facts, visions and action.

[21] Garry Wills, *Lincoln at Gettysburg: The Words that Remade America* (New York: Simon and Schuster, 1992) pp. 38-40.

[22] Ibid., p. 20. Italics mine.

[23] Herbert G. May and Bruce M. Metzger, ed. *The New Oxford Annotated Bible and Aocrypha: Revised Standard Version* (New York: Oxford University Press, 1977) p. 573.

[24] Thomas Cahill, *Desire of the Everlasting Hills: The World Before and After Jesus* (New York: Random House, 1999) pp. 22-30.

[25] Ibid., pp. 30,31.

Chapter 5: Jesus and Partnership Ways

[1] Most translations translate the Greek word BASILEIA as kingdom. This word is used in Mark and Matthew and is normally translated "kingdom" of God or "kingdom" of heaven. I translate it as rule. In my opinion, the reason that BASILEIA was translated as "kingdom" is because a kingdom was the only sort of government or rule known to those who were doing the translating. This reflects the prejudice of the dominator system. The fact is that what Jesus says about the so-called kingdom of God is a far cry from any sort of monarchy. According to Jesus' own descriptions of the rule of God, it is not accurate to describe God's rule as a monarchy. This is why I refuse to use the word kingdom as most translators do. Translating BASILEIA as rule leaves the style of governance open. Monarchy and Kingdom are clearly words that reflect our subjection of the dominator system. They should not be imposed on Jesus.

[2] Elaine Pagels, *The Gnostic Gospels* (New York: Vintage Books, 1979) p. xv, p. 22.

[3] Ibid. p. 49.

[4] Eisler, p. xvii.

[5] Joachim Jeremias, *The Parables of Jesus* (New York: Charles Scribner's Sons, 1972) pp. 70-77.

[6] Quinn, *Ishmael*, p. 125-148.

[7] See Michael Polanyi, *Personal Knowledge: Towards a Post-Critical Philosophy* (Chicago: University of Chicago Press, 1974) contends that all of knowledge, including scientific knowledge, is like this. It is never final. There is always more to it than we can tell.

[9] See George Orwell, *1984* (New York: Harcourt Bruce, 1949, 1977) for examples of a fictional account of the dominator system's desire to control language and thought as well as action.

[10] Enriche Dussell, *Ethics and Community,* translated by Robert R. Barr, (Maryknoll, New York: Orbis Books, 1988) gives an excellent account of the difference between ethics and morality. I believe I am following this account in the analysis that follows.

[11] Ibid, p. 49.

[12] Bernard Loomer, "Two Kinds of Power," *Criterion* 15, no. 1. (Winter 1976) p. 14.

[13] Ibid., p. 16.

[14] Peter J. Paris, *Social Teaching of the Black Churches* (Philadelphia: Fortress Press, 1985) p. 114.

[15] Ibid., p. 115.

[16] Ibid, p 118.

[17] Ibid., p. 118.

Chapter 6: Living in the Spirit of Jesus

[1] The Torah has also been called the Law of Moses in this work. The Torah is the first five books of what Christians call the Old Testament. Thus, in his effort to reinterpret the Torah, Paul was developing a way to interpret Scripture. The interpretations he opposes were those of the Pharisees. They are far more legalistic and literal in their interpretation of the Torah than Paul, but far less legalistic than many modern literalists believe themselves to be.

[2] This is how the dominator system solved the problem Paul presented. In effect, theologians were only fitting Paul into the framework of the dominator system. This could be done only by doing great injustice to Paul.

[3] Quinn, *My Ishmael*, p. 130-145.

[4] Quinn, *Providence*, p. 89.

[5] Paris, p. 118.

[6] It is important to note at least in passing that the word "hierarchy" combines the two Greek words for priest and first.

[7] Pagels, p. 34-35, 59-60, 114.

Chapter 7: Resisting the Dominator System

[1] Cantor, p. 5.

[2] Scott Gustafson, "The Scandal of Particularity and the Universality of Grace," *Religious Traditions and the Limits of Tolerance* (Chambersburg, Pa.: Anima Publications, 1988) pp. 24, 25.

[3] See Matthew 20: 1-15.

[4] Martin Hengel, *Crucifixion in the Ancient World and the Folly of the Message of the Cross* (Philadelphia: Fortress Press, 1977) p. 33.

[5] Ernest Kasemann, *Perspectives on Paul,* translated by Margaret Kohl (Philadelphia: Fortress Press, 1971) p. 36.

[6] Quinn, *Beyond Civilization*, p. 97.

[7] Charles Eastmann, *The Soul of the Indian* (Boston: Houghton Mifflin, 1911) pp. 119-120, as quoted Deloria, pp. 84, 85.

[8] Deloria, p. 87.

[9] Quinn, *Beyond Civilization*, p. 97.

[10] See Brueggemann, *Hopeful Imagination, Prophetic Imagination, Finally Comes the Poet: Daring Speech for Proclamation* (Minneapolis: Fortress Press, 1989), for many illustrations of the power of poetry to undermine the sterile, one dimensional words of the dominator system.

[11] Brueggemann, *Hopeful Imagination* pp. 53-55.

[12] The United States has killed as many civilians in Afghanistan as the terrorists killed at the World Trade Center. Chalmers Johnson, *The*

Sorrows of Empire: Militarism, Secrecy, and the End of the Republic (New York: Henry Holt and Company, 2004) p. 79. Johnson uses numerous citations from newspapers, the internet and scholarly journals in support of this claim. n. 29, p. 325. The United Nations estimates that 5000 people were killed by U.S. bombing, and perhaps 20,000 people died due to the disruption caused by the bombing.

[13] Noam Chomsky, *Hegemony or Survival: America's Quest for Global Dominance* (New York: Metropolitan Books, 2003) pp. 98-105.

[14] Ibid, p. 206, 207

[15] Wink, *The Powers That Be,* pp. 161-179.

[16] As told by Chai Ling's deputy Li Lu at the Albert Einstein Institution Conference on Non-Violent Sanctions for the National Defense. Boston, MA: February 10, 1990 as cited Wink, *Engaging the Powers*, pp. 141 – 142.

[17] Richard Deats, "Journey into Asia," *Fellowship* 56 (1990), as cited Wink, p. 142. See also Johnson, p. 70.

[18] Dorothy Soelle, *Suffering,* translated by Everett Kalin (Philadelphia: Fortress Press, 1975) p. 68.

[19] Wink, *Engaging the Powers*, p.166.

[20] Paris, pp. 114, 115.

[21] Ibid, p. 115.